G.I.G.G.L.E.S.

Girls In God Giving, Loving, Encouraging, Serving

She Laughs

Proverbs 31:25

Dr. Kristi L. Burk

G.I.G.G.L.E.S . . . She Laughs

Girls In God Giving Loving Encouraging Serving

Cover design and illustrations by Ravi R

Email: Dr.Kristyle@gmail.com

Library of Congress Control Number (LCCN) 2025900030
ISBN 979-8-218-78190-3

Audience: Ages 18+

10 9 8 7 6 5 4 3 2 1

1. Spiritual 2. Journal 3. Self-Help

First Printing

Printed in Morrow, Georgia United States of America

Acknowledgements

F irst I would like to thank God who is my strength and the head of my life. There are plenty of days that I wanted to throw in the towel with my book journey, but through prayer and God's grace, He gave me strength and wisdom to continue the journey. To my one and only son, Kah'lil Wade, I love you more than words can express. You are my knight, my light, and the reason I go hard in the paint every day! Through all our tests and trials, we both prevailed and I could not be any more thankful that God chose me to be your mother!

To my family and friends, thank you for your patience, support, and prayers. You all have been instrumental and loving in so many chapters of my life and this book journey. In addition, I want to shout out a special thanks to my awesome encouragement squad: Patricia Burk, Calvin Johnson, Deborah Williams, Heidi Griffin, Rhonda Skeaton, Keanna Skeaton, Stephanie Wood, Rachel Wood, Ruby Griffea, Kalita Griffea, Valerie Howard, Meda Brittman, Carolyn Anthony, Rene Moorer, Grizell Anthony, LaCrisha Darling, Shakinah "Necy" Barnett, Cheryl Travis-Jones, and Talisia King (photos by KodakbyTee) - you all know the roles you played in this journey and I am grateful you were on this ride with me!

I would like to thank Marcus Williams (Nubian Bookstore) for taking the time to discuss my book, sharing his insight and knowledge, and referring me to my publisher/book mentor. Finally, a special thanks to Kimberly Luttery! Within a short time, we clicked. You have been an awesome and knowledgeable mentor during my book publishing journey, and I can't thank you enough!
Love & Blessings!

Dr. Kristi L. Burk

Preface

My grandmother never had to tell us to get up. Our little bodies perked up to the smell of homemade pancakes, the sound of frying bacon, and the slight cracking of eggs on Sunday mornings. We knew like clockwork; breakfast, get dressed for church, get our quarter for church offering, and head down to Union Baptist Church. We would pile up in one pew and share a hymnal book. We giggled and sang off key until we were dismissed for Sunday School. After Sunday School is what we kids thought was nap time...the Sermon. Although grandma would give us a good swift pop on the head to sit up and pay attention, I'm not sure we ever really knew why we had to sit and listen to that guy in the black robe whoop and holler about a man named Jesus. Regardless, we were there every Sunday.

As we got older, we began to attend our uncle's church. We were the ushers, the choir, the congregation, the help, and any other positions we were needed for. As those teen years came along, some of us got a bit big for our pants. We wandered off into the world leaving our foundation to cry out for our return. For me, I was about 25 years old before I marched my wretched self-back to the church house. I made it a point to rekindle my belief and faith, not only for me, but for my son. Leaving the world behind and teaching my son the path of righteousness became my ultimate goal. We eventually landed in a church that nurtured both he and I. I became ordained, he was baptized, and we were thriving.

With our thriving came the tests and trials. I relied heavily on my spirituality and relationship with God. I also shared and testified what

I had gone through and how God had brought me out. Through it all, I discovered that my gift from God was to encourage and teach.

I started a study group, a blog, and an online prayer group. The groups and blogs were successful in encouraging and assisting with learning the Bible.

For a few years, I would get up every morning bright and early (as if I smelled pancakes) and read the Bible. I would then jot down what came to mind, and this is how the blog started. I had a couple of people join my blog, and they were so enlightened with the material that they encouraged me to do more with it. I then started the online prayer group that encouraged reading & studying the bible, healthy eating, good stewardship over finances, and how to bridle the tongue.

The word got around, and I found that I had acquaintances that were not comfortable within the church walls but wanted to learn and receive the Word. This is when I started a Bible study in my home. Every Thursday for a couple hours, I would run through lessons and discussion about the Bible. This Bible study grew as the weeks went on. Eventually, life took me down another path and the online prayer group became the focus of lessons and encouragement.

One year turned into two, and then three, and before you knew it, I had a compilation of Bible lessons and writings that encouraged women throughout our city and a few other states.

The material that you will read in this book is the very material that nurtured and encouraged my study and prayer groups. The first and second chapters are my reflections of the books of Psalms and Proverbs, and the third chapter is a reflection of different scriptures or writings that I shared with my groups.

The excerpts are thoughts of the heart that were inspired by God. Some of them are bold and straight to the point, while others will tickle you to giggle. Some of the writings/posts are duplicates but relative. Overall, the sharing of God's Word was the goal, and the sharing was from my heart, my point of view, and how I felt God led me.

Now I'm sharing my posts and writings in book form. You never know who can benefit from your story, testimony, or ideas.

To God be the Glory!

1

Walking Through Psalms

As I studied the Bible, I shared with others. I challenge YOU to share and encourage someone.

Several years ago I started a BlogSpot that I shared with women who needed encouragement and an accountability partner to ensure daily Bible reading. During my Bible reading, I would read one chapter of a book per day and share my thoughts or lessons to be learned in this blog. I walked through the book of Psalms and encouraged women to read the daily chapter, share in my thoughts, and develop their own thoughts, responses, or takeaways from the reading.

I encouraged them to develop a reading and study plan for the book of Psalms. In addition, I requested that they reflect from the following passages to invoke further thought, gain a lesson, or simply giggle and delight in the passages.

Let the Psalms begin...

Psalm 1

Short and sweet...the life of the faithful or the life of the faithless? Which are you? We claim to want more of God, yet we waddle in sin proclaiming change with our mouths and no action. Scripture tells us exactly what we should be doing, delight in the Lord and meditate on His Word day and night, yet some choose the other path that ultimately leads to destruction. No gray areas. It's black or white. Do you choose to be lost in the dark or live abundantly in the glorious light?

Peace and Blessings

Psalm 2

How much do you really want God in your life? Psalm 2 speaks of surrendering to God and to stop trying to operate in one's own strength. We must begin to look to God who is almighty and all-powerful. The things we do in life are nothing if we don't have God in it. We must recognize and begin to trust God in all that we do or say.

We must stand firm on what we know and learn about God not to be bamboozled by any wind of doctrine, action, or misinterpretation. We are to be heavyweights in God, not lightweights that can be carried off by the wind. Seek God with your heart and confess with your mouth that He is Lord. Try Him and you will see, nothing is as good or satisfying as our God, and only He can cover All!

Peace and Blessings

Psalm 3

Feeling all alone? Feel that everyone or the world is against you? Well, God's grace, mercy, and compassion is sufficient for our well-being. Trusting in God is an attribute we must become intimate with. Trust is built and when it is betrayed, it is hard to get back to the point of thorough trust. God said He would never leave us nor forsake us. He also said to abide by His Word, so when we go through or feel alone, remember we serve an awesome God that is totally trustworthy, and He is always there for us. We must also do our part in our relationship with God. We must live right, call on Him in our every word or move, and when things come up against us, no worries, the God in us will be strong enough to handle any situation. Even when the situation seems grim, we have God.

There is nobody like Him!

Peace and Blessings

Psalm 4

God knows what we need. He also knows what we are inquiring about in our prayer before we even pray it. Therefore, we must go to God right. God is the ultimate protector and provides grace and peace.

We can go to God anytime - anywhere. Our communication with God is never limited unless we have caused the limitation.

When we have or done said things outside of the Will of God, we will reap the consequences of our actions or words, but our God is so

awesome, He forgives, and we must become loyal to Him as He is to us. Speak with God daily. Use your prayer life to unfold the mysteries of life. Build a strong connection with God and you will never have to worry about the trials of the world coming against you. You will have peace and rest in God's Word trusting in Him only, and He shall direct your path, order your steps, and keep you from all hurt, harm, or danger.

Peace and Blessings

Psalm 5

Verse 3 is a request for God to hear our prayer in the morning. Why in the morning? This is when our minds are more clear and less occupied. We can commit to our communion or time spent praying with less distractions. The scripture goes on to say how sin should not be tolerated and will not be tolerated by God, not even the "smallest" sin. We must recognize the sin in our lives and begin to CHANGE from those sinful ways and thoughts. We must become committed to daily prayer, reading of the Word, and begin to shed off all of our sinful ways or thoughts. Make time, MAKE TIME, make time for GOD and reduce the time invested in sinful ways or thoughts. Pray daily about everything. Pray daily about everything. Pray daily about everything.

Repetition makes for a well-rounded child of God.

Peace and Blessings

Psalm 6

When we recognize that we have sinned, we must go to God for forgiveness. We must pray that God is merciful and gracious in His forgiving. Just because we have a God of second chances and a God that is willing to provide brand new mercies every day does not allow us to continue to sin.

There is no "sin" pass. We must learn to stay on that straight and narrow path of righteousness and deter ourselves from ALL sin. When we have sinned, we must go to God with a sincere heart and pray for forgiveness that only He can grant. Be open and honest with God (He knows anyway) and begin to purify your heart, thoughts, and actions. Don't be a victim of circumstances, but a child of God that can receive forgiveness.

Peace and Blessings

Psalm 7

When we feel we have been done wrong, or feel the need to take revenge, we can carry out our actions in our own strength, OR we can go to God. God is our ultimate fighter and protector. There will always be trials or situations that come up against us, whether we like it or not, and whether we admit it or not, and instead of carelessly trying to handle it ourselves, go to God in prayer.

FAST. Seek wisdom, LET GO AND LET GOD. God knows all, He knows your every thought, your every motive, your every move, your everything. Nothing comes as a surprise to God; remember He knew you before you were in your mother's womb. So when you feel troubled, God allows His love, grace, and mercy to be extended to you. I know, I heard you. Sometimes you feel God does not hear or answer your prayers. The truth is you must have a REAL and tight relationship with God. He is not a microwave God where you can come to Him or use Him quick, fast, and in a hurry.

God wants a relationship with you through the good and the bad. So, when you feel that God is distant and prayers are not answered, draw closer to God through reading and praying. He will never leave you nor forsake you, but you must do your part in the relationship.

Father God, I pray that You heal any heavy hearts, give us comfort and understanding that is beyond human measure. Have us to seek You in all things, have us to stay on the path of righteousness, protect us from our enemies, and guide us in the way You want us to go. Father God, as we move through our day, help us to be a light to those who don't know You or an influence on those who have fallen short. Speak life into our thoughts and actions; and we thank You Lord! We thank You for Your grace

and mercy; we thank You Lord for keeping us during the night and as we wake up in the morning; we thank You Lord that our good days will outweigh our bad days. WE WON'T COMPLAIN! We trust You and honor You. THANK YOU LORD. WE WON'T COMPLAIN!

Peace and Blessings

Psalm 8

This scripture brings back the memories of when I was a youth singing in my uncle's church choir at New Haven. Sandi Patty had a tape out and she sang: O Lord, our Lord, how majestic is Your name in all the Earth! O Lord, our Lord, how majestic is Your name in all the Earth! O Lord, we praise Your name, O Lord, we magnify Your name, Prince of peace, mighty God, O Lord, God, almighty!

Man! That was some good praising. Think about those words. Think about Chapter 8 and how God created all, how He allows us to rule and roam the Earth, how God gave us Jesus for our salvation, how God gives us choice, how God gives us grace and mercy, how

God gives us strength, O Lord, God almighty!

Peace and Blessings

Psalm 9

Give God praise! For He has done great things! Reflect on all of your blessings, the troubles He has brought you through, and the comfort He has given you. God is so awesome. He deserves our praise every minute of the day. Begin to show God your appreciation by giving Him praise every day! When you wake, let God know how you adore Him, how you appreciate Him waking you up every morning, giving you the use of your limbs, being kept from ailments, and all things that He has or can do for you. Not only does God deserve our praise for blessing us, but He is our protector. God can protect us from ANYTHING. He keeps us from our enemies, He saves us from damnation, He never leaves us when we feel lost or suffering.

God created us in His likeness; therefore, we must not get caught up in this world, but get caught up in the "what would Jesus do" mentality. God delights in seeing His creations do as He instructs, live as He instructs, and communing with Him as He instructs.

Allow God into your heart, let Him into your daily prayer, let God move in you that His ways become your ways, His words become your words, and above all, LOVE.

Thank You Lord God for waking us in the morning! Thank You Lord for the reading of Your Word, that we may conform to Your ways and begin to look more like You!

Thank You Lord for every breath we take and every move we make. I pray that You continue to be the guide of our lives and bless us according to Your Will. We pray for our families, friends, employers, coworkers, those who have lost loved ones, our government, the weak, the needy, those who don't know You, and our enemies.

Protect us from all hurt, harm, and danger and keep us under Your loving care. Thank You Jesus, for we are nothing without You. Thank You for Your saving grace, thank You for brand new mercies every day, thank You that we need nothing more than You! Thank You Jesus, AMEN!

Peace and Blessings

Psalm 10

Christians and those who try to live right always seem to wonder why unbelievers and the wicked seem to do well and get ahead. Well, no need to wonder, nothing goes unseen by God. He knows and sees all. God has a plan for each and every one of us. Never set your sights on someone else, but keep your eyes and mind set on God. What God has for you is for you and He can do all things possible. Stop dwelling on others and rely on God. When we grow in our faith and mature in our faith, God will reward us with blessings and the desires of our heart.

Keep God first in all things you do. God loves you and so do I!

Peace and Blessings

Psalm 11

Psalm 11 piggybacks Psalm 10. The wicked is still hard at work and doing their corrupt ways, but no fear, God is still in control. God watches and protects. We must believe in Him and not waver. The enemy may seem strong but the God in us makes us stronger. So, when we are feeling overwhelmed or begin to question our spiritual freedom, remember that God has not and will not leave us nor forsake us.

Trust in Him with all thine heart, give Him praise in everything; tighten up your relationship with God; and live according to His Word. Pray for those who don't know our God. Pray for those who are caught up in wicked ways. Pray for guidance. Pray for yourself. Pray To God. God loves His children!

Peace and Blessings

Psalm 12

Living for God in a wicked world seems unbearable sometimes. The temptations, lies, deceitfulness, and evil may crowd our spiritual being leaving us to feel alone in this world or without God. Well, fret no more, the devil is under our feet. God is awesome in that He gives us an outlet for everything. When we feel pushed into a corner or lonely, we can seek out other believers to give us guidance and support; and we can call on the name of Jesus to mend our broken heart or thoughts. We must become sincere in our spiritual walk; live in truth that we can fight any battle; For God so love the world, He sent His only begotten Son – this alone is enough for us to STRAIGHTEN up. Begin to evaluate your life, make changes that are conducive to the Word, let God's Word fight your battles, and let the Spirit lead you. Pray over your family, our situations, our country, employers, government, friends coworkers, and enemies. Seek to do your part in God's army. Trust in the Lord with all thine heart.

Rest in the peace of the Lord.

Peace and Blessings

Psalm 13

The word for the day is "patience". We must exhibit patience when we are waiting on affirmation from God. God knows what is best for us and when He should move with us. When we are dealing with something or going through something, we want God to handle it in a microwave minute. Well, our God is not a microwave. He is an on-time God and He moves when He sees fit. If you feel you've been waiting too long to hear from Him or you become impatient, CHECK YOURSELF. God is almighty and never makes a mistake. Trust in Him wholeheartedly and stand firm in your faith, God can, and God will. Learn to speak those things as though they are.

Stop dwelling in negativity and jolt your Spirit with songs of praise. Read your Bible and revive yourself. We are not losers, we are not defeated, we will not have our lights snuffed out, and we will not have our joy taken. We are children of the most high God, we are victorious, we will let our light shine, and this joy we have, NO one can take away! Repent, ask for forgiveness, pray for all, love life, and seek God in everything!

Peace and Blessings

Psalm 14

Sometimes we get caught up in this world; being caught up in this world leads us to fall short or lose sight of our spirituality. We must remember our true purpose here on Earth. God has called us to be a witness, to be Christ-like, to follow His Word, and to love one another. How can we do this in such a corrupt world? By holding onto God's unchanging hand! We must put away our old ways and let the new man begin to do his work. We must recognize what is of God and what is not; we must encourage each other during the good and bad; we must not allow sin to fester in our lives, we must show affection towards others; and we must correct and guide the lost. We can do all things through the love of Christ, but we – WE – have to be willing. We must put action to these very words that you're reading right now. Think back…when was the last time you verbally encouraged someone? When was the last time you turned from a sin and DID NOT LOOK BACK? When was the last time you showed affection towards someone other than your mate or family? When was the last time you have rattled off scripture or God's awesomeness to someone? If it took longer than one minute to answer these questions, it's time! It's time to get on track and line up with God. God sees and knows all, and He is patiently waiting for your wholehearted arrival. WE cannot hide our thoughts, feelings, or actions from God. So, while you are living your everyday life, make God a big part of why you move, speak, and breathe. Make it clear to yourself, and others, who you serve by walking in your spirituality. Turn your life over to God and let Him lead you. There is not a devil in hell who can touch you when you serve God!

Peace and Blessings

Psalm 15

This chapter has a theme of "blameless life". Huh? Blameless?! That's right! Blameless! We are reminded over and over again how God created us in his own likeness; therefore, we are to strive to live right and bring Him joy. We should enter His courts with praise; go unto him with a clean heart; live according to His Word; speak the truth and veer from lies and gossip; refrain from sinning and doing evil; press through test and trials; and do right unto others. All of these things reflect a blameless life. When we are pure at heart and have a strong relationship with God, we can accomplish, press through, or see through anything that is set before us. We can speak life into every situation, someone's life, our own lives, and control the way we live. Words are powerful and like water in carpet; once it spills out, you can't take them back. So begin to speak over yourself, your family, friends, situations, employers, coworkers, our country, those with ailments, haters, fakers, and enemies; coupled with living by the Word, God can and will bless you for your obedience. Although we can never be perfect, blameless can be a goal.

Get right church! And make our Father proud!

Peace and Blessings

Psalm 16

When we trust in God and know who God is for ourselves, we can rest in knowing that everything we do or go through in life involves Him. We can go to God for anything, when we don't feel well, when we are suffering a loss, when we feel down and out, when we see corruption in others, when we are thankful, and when we want to give God praise and worship for just being Him. We serve a mighty God and He can provide security, hope, joy, confidence, and happiness. We gain these attributes by allowing God to dwell within us and obeying His Word. We can rejoice knowing that God gives us new mercies and grace every day. EVERY DAY. God does not hold a grudge; He gives us love. This alone is a reason to shout and praise Him every morning, every waking minute of the day!

To find this joy...seek God every day, and in everything you do. Pray without ceasing. Give God His due praise and worship, live life abundantly, enjoy the pleasures of life on Earth, spread the Good News, let your light shine, and let Jesus be the reason.

Peace and Blessings

Psalm 17

Life is full of ups and downs, happiness and sadness, good and evil; and because life seems to have repetition in this manner, God's Word continually guides us to deal with it all. In this lifetime, we will experience happy times, sad times, unspeakable joy, heartache, laughter, and some crying.

Sometimes when we experience the negative aspects of life, we feel God has failed or left us. Not so! God is always present and knows everything about our lives. Do you read your Bible every day? Do you study the Word every day? Do you pray every day? Do you congregate with like-minded people every day? If you answered "no" to one or more of these questions, do you think God feels you have failed or left Him? Did you catch on? This is a two-way street.

A relationship involves two that are connected or associated. In this instance, we must have a connection or association with God to gain knowledge, wisdom, and strength to handle any ups and downs life may bring us. We can go to God for everything, but we must have a consistent relationship with Him to advance us in our faith. He will always protect and provide; but He also wants You, me, US to be responsible in the call on our lives. When up, give Him praise; when down, dig deep to draw on your faith and give Him praise. Stop dwelling and become mature in your faith and handle negative aspects in faith. Learn to pray unceasingly, read the Word daily, study the Word, pray before you do anything, expect God, turn from sin, speak life, and do unto others as you would have them do unto you. We serve an awesome God and He adores you! God will protect you from enemies and a broken heart, but you must line up and show God that you appreciate Him, love and adore Him. Then He will give you the desires of your heart.

Peace and Blessings

Psalm 18

God is our protector. God is our savior; God keeps us. God is almighty. God is our fortress. God gives us victory. God is our everything. GOD IS! As long as we got King Jesus, we don't need nobody else! When all is well, God's got us. When all seems grim, God's got us.

There is not a situation or issue that is a surprise to God or that He can't handle. When we follow God with all our heart, He will bless us. He gave us His only begotten Son to save our ratchet lives. God wants us to invest in Him more than we invest in anything else. Your mother, your father, your brother, your sister, your mate, your child, or your friends...none can compare to Him! Take up your cross and walk with your head up. Represent God for the mighty one that He is, so that no one can be confused that you are His. Speak those things as though they are, for we are never defeated! Submit to the Word, get Satan under your feet; God said He would make our enemies our footstool as long as we keep Him first. Stop putting all your efforts in worldly ways and begin to exhibit God in your walk, talk, actions, and decisions. Never get discouraged, for God is not a god of confusion, nor does He give in or lose.

Reflect the characteristics of God, make every day a God day. When we live right, God will bless us!

Peace and Blessings

Psalm 19

May the words of my mouth and the meditation of my heart be pleasing to you, O Lord, my rock and my redeemer (v14). I encourage you to meditate on this scripture. Get it in your heart and soul.

Peace and Blessings

Psalm 20

God is the creator of all Heaven and Earth. When we indulge in what God has created here on Earth, we can see His mighty handiwork. The beautiful skies, the radiant sun, twinkling stars, flowing trees, waves of the sea, and so many more creations that could only be the work of our God. Not only must we delight in what God has created for our pleasure, we must delight in Him and His Word. With His Word and graciousness, we are filled with His healing power, knowledge, and wisdom. Life is what we make it, and it can be very short-lived without Him. Make the most of what God has for you and follow through. Love all who God is and what He can provide.

Pray for a clean heart, wisdom, comfort, and guidance...live according to His Word!

Peace and Blessings

Psalm 21

We must be thankful for all that we are and have. We woke up this morning, we have use of our senses and limbs, we have our families, jobs, a roof over our heads, food on the table, transportation, etc. These things are possible because of God. We must stand firm in our trust and love for God, that trials, tribulations, or events in our lives, don't sway us from standing our ground. We must recognize and confirm from what we believe and allow God to be the head of our lives and battles. We will not always understand why God allows or does certain things, but we must be strong in our faith, love, and in His Word that we can

withstand any trials or darts that may come our way. We are victorious in battle – meaning we fight worldly battles with the Word – or – we put God first in everything – or – we are holding tight to God's unchanging hand, especially when we don't understand. God wants our attention, He wants a regular relationship, He wants us to strive to be upright and live according to His Word, and when we make these efforts, He is content. God delights in His children and will bless them accordingly. So when you wake up every day, give Him praise.

When you have a breakthrough, give Him praise. When you have prayed for someone, give Him praise. When you have helped someone, give Him praise. When someone has helped you, give Him praise. Give Him praise in everything! We are victorious!

Peace and Blessings

Psalm 22

This world can be very "cold!" We experience heartache, backstabbing disappointment, ignorance, hatred, liars, confusion, and trials. We waddle through these times feeling that they will never end. We try to ease the pressure with drugs, alcohol, gossip, lashing out, or having a pity party. When we experience any type of suffering, we must turn to God. Sometimes, God allows long-suffering, so if you choose the wrong path to get through "cold" times, it may take you longer to become pure from the fire. On the other hand, we can look to the hills which cometh our help. We can seek God during these times of suffering and know that any test He allows only matures us in faith. We can rely on God's Word that we will always be victorious in any situation. WHY? Because His Word says so. God will never leave nor forsake us. We must learn to endure and press on. We must rely on our prayer life and allow God to work in us. IN HIS TIMING. God loves us very much and we must learn to reciprocate the same love.

God acknowledges this love we are to reciprocate in our reading of His Word, through our communication of prayer, through our help toward others, and through our praise and worship. There is a praise in our breakthroughs. Know that you will go through, know that God will see you through, and know that the victory is already ours. Be strong! Read God's Word daily. Study God's Word that it may fester in your soul. Give God daily praise and worship. PRAY, PRAY, PRAY. Love life and don't live defeated. Giving God honor is what we do!

Peace and Blessings

Psalm 23

Many people are familiar with Psalm 23. This is one of the most popular scriptures and can be reflected upon in many situations. In addition, this scripture is more than likely the most memorized scripture in the Bible. Today, we will focus on the very first verse...The Lord is my Shepherd. A shepherd provides guidance and care for his sheep; thus God provides care and spiritual guidance for His children. I encourage you to do a little study regarding sheep. A small tidbit – a sheep's eyes are on the side of its head, and they usually flock together. By the eyes being on the side of the head, their vision is obstructed, and they cannot see head-on, and in this instance, they will follow what they see around them...other sheep. If other sheep are veering off or not following the guidance of the Shepherd or his staff, they get lost, fall off, or get into trouble. This is why sheep have a shepherd, to guide them in which way to go, to steer them to the appropriate place to graze, and to protect them from danger. Sound familiar?

The second sentence of the verse sums it up - I shall not want. This is because God is our guidance, and we have all that we need with Him. God is so good, He gives us encouragement, guidance, love, grace, and mercy in every word we read in this scripture. Study the scripture and understand why it is the most popular scripture, then give God His due praise and worship.

Peace and Blessings

Psalm 24

Everything belongs to God... the Heavens, the Earth, and the fullness thereof. We need to reflect on the detail of everything...the

blinking of the eye, the smell of a flower, the song of a bird, the warm breeze of the wind, the whisper of a loved one...things we rarely give thought to are the creations of God. We must begin to appreciate every aspect of life and speak optimistically of all things and situations. When we open our hearts and minds to God, we allow Him to come in and dwell peacefully in our temples. When God open doors for us, He allows grace, mercy, love, and the desires of our hearts. We are strong in God and He in us. Sing praises unto the Lord always. Allow Him to work and use you in the way He sees fit, don't get discouraged, keep pressing, for God has and will continue to do wonderful things. The Lord is strong and mighty. We too, are strong and mighty when we follow Him and reflect on "everything" that is of Him.

Thank You Jesus for the blood, thank You Jesus for removing our sins, thank You Jesus that we can call You friend, thank You Jesus for this day and every day. We honor and worship You! Amen!

Peace and Blessings

Psalm 25

As children of God, we are constantly faced with a temptation and the work of the enemy. As children of God, we are equipped to be victorious over any temptation and the enemy. David, the man after God's own heart, wrote many of the Psalms and he always cried out to God for guidance and wisdom.

We must learn from David and stay consistent in how we communicate and call on God. We must recognize those things that may come up against us and seek God in how to deal with each and every situation. We must be faithful unto God and not act as a fair-weathered friend, for God is the only one who can turn spiraling drama into glorious victories.

Like many of David's Psalms and prayers, we must continue to seek God in everything. Ask God for daily guidance and wisdom. Ask God to help us stay on the straight and narrow path to righteousness. Ask God to give us courage and stand up against trials or tribulations. Ask God to grow and mature us in our faith. Seek God and ask God.

Continue to build your prayer life. Give God His due time with you. Read the Bible and show yourself approved. Press to live according to His Word. Share the love of God, and in all that you do – Pray!

Peace and Blessings

Psalm 26

When we confess with our mouths that Jesus is Lord and believe that God has raised Him from the dead, we are saved (Romans 10:9). This relationship between us and God is now bonded. God has forgiven us and provided us with salvation. In return, how do you thank God for such an awesome gift?

Answer: loyalty and commitment.

We must begin to shed off our own ways and set our sights on God's Word. Our motivation should be to have a clean heart, to become more and more like Christ, and to live without sin. I know, I know, no one is perfect, and we all fall short. However, living with integrity and keeping ourselves away from sinful influences shows God that we are willing. When we are willing, God can examine our true motives and our hearts. He knows what is stirring up deep down inside, and when things come up against us, He knows how we will react. So make our Father proud. Live according to the Word and get your motives in check.

When necessary, learn how to be around unbelievers and not sin, but be of encouragement. Be a brighter light for someone who may be snuffed out or have no light at all. Collectively, when we live right, seek God in all things and give God praise, we can live abundantly here on Earth. We receive grace and mercy every day and we can stand firm in knowing we are victorious in everything because we have King Jesus. Are you loyal to God?

Peace and Blessings

Psalm 27

We should have no fear because of who we are in Christ and who Christ is in us. We all have been some type of prisoner to fear. However, we can conquer fear by trusting in the Lord – the light of our salvation. We must also be

confident. We must be confident in what we read and know about God and His Word, stand firm on it and not waiver. When we feel we are lying in wait for God's response, or we feel He has not heard or answered our cries, we must trust and remain confident, not only that God hears us, but that we know He will show up. When feeling overwhelmed, God will show up. When sad or lonely, God will show up. When you don't understand, God will show up. When you feel like throwing in the towel, God will show up. Never give up on God because He will never give up on you. Patience is a virtue. Waiting for God is not easy, but when He is ready and shows up, that will be the time of refreshing. Stay obedient, stay in His Word. Believe, pray, press forward, and never give up. God loves you!

Peace and Blessings

Psalm 28

Over and over King David prayed unto the Lord. When surrounded by trouble, he prayed to the Lord.

When things went wrong, he prayed to the Lord. When feeling alone, he prayed to the Lord. David has set the example; God is our source of safety and comfort. God will protect His children. When we pray to God, we must be straightforward and sincere when we pray. God already knows our hearts and motives. Therefore, we are not to sugarcoat how we feel or what we pray about. Go to the Father with a voice of strength, for we are not weak but strong. Communicate with God in confidence and allow Him to move in your life. Build that close relationship with God that can be called "friendship."

Our relationship with God should not be fair-weathered, but lasting and strong. Do not allow evil, wickedness, and sin to creep in and taint your very being or relationship with God. Do as David did... PRAY!

Peace and Blessings

Psalm 29

After reading the scripture this morning, one song comes to mind;

"there is power, power, wonder working power, in the blood of the lamb, there is power, power, wonder working power in the precious blood of the lamb." The power! The power of God is unmistakable. When He speaks all things move or tremble. God's voice controls all creation. He can speak to the wind and sea, and they will be still. He raised Jesus from the dead, and He lives. If our God can do all these things, can't His voice give us strength to move through anything? God is available to us, seek Him!

Peace and Blessings

Psalm 30

Choose God! Rely on Him solely. God is our guidance, protector, and Savior. Only God, ONLY God can do what no other can. Trust in Him always. Any situation, any circumstance, any trial, any tribulation, God can see you through. Don't get caught up in material things or money, but wait on the Lord. Find your rest and peace in God.

Peace and Blessings

Psalm 31

We claim to have faith in God, but do we really trust Him? When we go through trials or tribulations, sometimes we try to handle the situations with our own strength and knowledge, and what happens? The plan backfires. We must commit ourselves to God, our vocations, our families, our possessions, and our prayer life. We must continue to rely on God for and in every aspect of our lives. We must learn and put into action what we read in the Bible and not just merely say, "we read it". We must study the Bible to get truth and meaning, we must memorize scripture to fight the battle of sin, and we must love one another. Through it all, love conquers all. God loved us enough to allow His Son to die on the cross, so in return, we must gain the wisdom the Bible provides us to live and love accordingly.

Peace and Blessings

Psalm 32

When we have sinned or done wrong, we may hold some guilt regarding that sin or wrongdoing. In an effort to shed that guilt, we must confess and repent. If we are bold enough to sin, we should be strong and bold enough to confess our sin. Once we have confessed, we must be even stronger to repent. TURN AWAY from sin, not merely tell God, "I won't do it again," but really make the effort to turn away from that very sin as to not repeat or go back to it. When we have confessed and repented, then ask God for forgiveness. God is willing to wipe our slates clean when we have taken the steps to recognize our wrongdoing, confessed with our mouths, and repent those ways. There is nothing too hard for God, so stop trying to do things in your own strength. Stop dabbling in the wrong things and expecting God to fix it right away. Learn to stand firm on His Word and to say NO TO SIN. Take ownership of your life and the way you live. Pray before making any decisions or taking actions.

Change things about yourself that will promote obedience and strive to live without sin. Carry your cross. Love with your whole heart and thank God for everything!

Peace and Blessings

Psalm 33

God is worthy of our praise and trust. God is faithful and dependable. We can put all our hope in God, and He will never fail us. When God spoke, the world began, therefore, when God speaks into our lives - whatever it is - all things are possible. We can rest assure that everything that is good and perfect comes from the Lord. We must continue to obey God's Word, and God will keep us under His watchful care and protection. Trust God, give God praise, rejoice in God, for He can never fail.

Peace and Blessings

Psalm 34

God is our everything. When we are obedient to His Word and live

accordingly, we can expect great things from God. He will set us free from our fears, guard and defend us, show us goodness, supply our needs, listen when we call on Him, and He forgives and redeems us. None of these things are a free ticket to sin, but just some of the joys God is willing to share with us when we live as He asks. We can show the Lord we love Him through deep respect, reverence, and honor.

Question for the day: How do you respect, reverence, and honor the Lord?

Peace and Blessings

Psalm 35

There will always be backstabbers, naysayers, haters, or the spiteful. When we know and trust God, we do not have to handle them in our own strength. We must pray and turn them over to God. When the wicked has come up against us, we can ask God to defend us, and we don't need to waste our time giving into their sin.

Remember that deliverance may not always be as immediate as we would want it, but when we give it to God, He will make our enemies our footstools. We must keep our heads up, pray for those that don't know better, ask God to intervene on our behalf, give God praise and thanks for all we go through, and leave doubt at the door! When we still feel all else has failed, we can find a place to seek God in deep meditation, get on our knees and pray, give God reverence, and depend solely on Him. When we trust and love God, we do not have to fight fleshly battles.

Peace and Blessings

Psalm 36

The wicked stir up evil and sinful ways. The wicked also have no restraint on how they sin or when they sin. Punishment for their sins seem far and few in between, but lo and behold, God will. Just when the wicked feel they have conquered in their quest, God will rise up and handle them. Do not fall into this trap. Fear God! God will punish the wicked and ungodly. Turn from sin, press to do what is right by God in His Word, stay on the straight and narrow path that leads to righteousness. God is faithful, and just. He knows what you struggle with, but when you choose the right path, He will ultimately reward you. Weigh your options, right or wrong...good or bad, sin or God?

Question: Do you prefer "right now satisfaction" or eternal life?

Peace and Blessings

Psalm 37

Good vs. evil. Instead of focusing on the things that are wicked or evil, the Word tells us to rely on God, trust in God, commit to God, wait on God, be slow to anger, do not lose your temper, stand against the wicked or evil, do not love money, care for the needy, offer good counsel, and be honest. As believers, we have many aspects of life in which we can spiritually or physically help others. We can also improve our own well-being by living righteously. That means engaging in the things mentioned above. We must not compare ourselves to others, what they do, or what they have; but live according to where God has placed us and what He has given us. Everything about our lives was written before we were in the womb. There is nothing we can do to change that; however, we can press to live according to His Word. Give God reverence by the way we live. He gave us free choice, and we should strive to make good choices.

Instead of giving up or giving in to those ways that are not of God – pray, confess, repent, and be forgiven. Choose "Good".

Peace and Blessings

Psalm 38

When we or someone close to us has sinned, we feel the pain or sorrow that the sin brings. Our hearts are heavy, our bodies are weighed down, and our thoughts are sporadic. When we turn to God and repent those sins, there is hope in the sorrow. The Word tells us we will reap what we sow. However, when we confess and ask for forgiveness for the sin committed, God will be the judge of the consequence to endure, or grant mercy and forgiveness. The wicked love to see Christians fall into sin and look for the chance to throw it in their face. Just as Jesus stood silent to His accusers, we can stay silent to those that gossip or encourage sin. We must commune with God and allow Him to hear our hearts, our confessions, and then He can and will work out the consequences for our sins.

Continue to trust and have faith in God and His Word, because you can only grow stronger. Remember that everything you go through can be a lesson learned, but you have to identify the lesson and LEARN from it.

Don't waddle in the mess. Allow God to bless you!

Peace and Blessings

Psalm 39

Live life to the fullest. We must learn to overcome sin and obstacles and to live happily. Everyone's days are numbered, and only God knows when our time will expire. In this instance, we must become immune to sin, wicked ways, and watch our tongues. These attributes contribute to wrong living and can stunt our spiritual growth or block our blessings. When we love and trust God, we can get through anything and live a life of joy while here on Earth. Take time to make necessary changes in your life that would allow you to grow spiritually, live comfortably, and give God glory.

Peace and Blessings

Psalm 40

To receive blessings, we must wait on the Lord. We must go through trials and be patient as God works out the aspects of our lives. Learning to endure, engaging in continual obedience, and being of good faith sets us on the path to be blessed.

Allow God to move in your life. Take delight in His Word and what He has for you. Draw closer to God so that you may know and understand how you hear His voice. As you continue to work on your relationship with God, share with others what you do know or your growing experience. God is faithful... Are you?

Peace and Blessings

Psalm 41

The Bible prepares us for some of our worst times. When we are sick or experiencing ailments, when we have become the center of gossip, when we have been abandoned or betrayed by the very ones we trust, we must learn seek God and use His Word to handle these situations. When going through anything, we must lean on God for understanding, wisdom, healing, and direction. God will explain the misunderstood. God will lead the blind. God can cure any hurt, pain, or ailment. God will show you the path of righteousness. Pray for God's grace and mercy over everything you do, and in your life. Build up strong faith and continue to pray for the enemy. Find peace and trust in God. Get rid of the sour attitude. Do not waver. Do not give in. Do not let go. Be strong. Stay encouraged. Fight battles with the Word. Show thyself approved and live abundantly.

Peace and Blessings

Psalm 42

As children of God, we must rely on God for everything; for our sound mind, for decisions, how we behave, how we speak, how we live, and how we interact with others. We need God. When we are lonely, we can reach out to God. When we are depressed, we can communicate with God. When we are confused, we can read God's Word. We need God.

Peace and Blessings

Psalm 43

Sometimes our troubles weigh us down. Sometimes we feel God is not there to see us through the situation. Sometimes we feel God has not heard our prayers, and sometimes we just feel defeated. Why?

Although God would NEVER leave nor forsake us, God will allow us to go through long-suffering to build up our faith. Sometimes we have to go through the fire to come out pure as gold. God does not sleep. God does not trick you. God does not leave you hanging. God deserves our faithfulness and loyalty. God observes our commitment. God observes our maturity. God delights in our victory over sin, drama, and temptations. God will also allow us to take this journey through life and it might seem He is not there, but God is always there watching His precious children and smiling at accomplishments. God is proud to see His children grow and press through weary times. Never think that God is not there or that He doesn't care, He just allows us to demonstrate our loyalty and faith to Him, keep pressing!

Peace and Blessings

Psalm 44

Going through something? Got struggles? Feeling some kind of way? Depression? Stress? Tired? Stay strong! Call on God! Pray! Hallelujah, ANYHOW!

Peace and Blessings

Psalm 45

The bride of Christ is the church. We are the church, precious, anointed, and chosen. All that is good and surrounds us is of God's blessings. Because God has identified us as the bride of Christ, we shall give Him praise and worship all the days of our lives. God delights in the chosen, and we shall honor Him in our faith, loyalty, and commitment. Love Christ as He loves us. Be free of committing adultery and sinful ways that we may be showered with the love of God.

Peace and Blessings

Psalm 46

Short and sweet, God is our strength in any circumstance. God is our refuge in the midst of it all.

Peace and Blessings

Psalm 47

God is the creator of all. He is our protector, our Savior, and everything in between. Reflect on everything that God has done for you, what He can do for you, and who He is to you. God is AWESOME. Give God praise!

Peace and Blessings

Psalm 48

Whatever life may bring; God is with us. When it seems that all walls are caving in on us, God is with us. When we have a breakthrough, God is with us. God is with us always and forever. Glorify Him!

Peace and Blessings

Psalm 49

Question: is your wealth here on Earth or in your faith?

When financial wealth is built up here on Earth, the wealthy tend to become comfortable in status and material things. There are

some things that money cannot buy. When we leave this Earth, we will leave without money, without expensive clothing, without cars, and without material things. If God has allowed us to be wealthy here on Earth, our focus should not be wrapped up in what we can bought or what can be paid for, but our faith should be growing in trust and understanding.
No matter what the financial situation, we must learn to grow in God's Word. Stay humble, know that God is always present, trust that His Word will prosper in our lives, and pray for daily guidance. We can become "rich" in mind; learn God's Word for ourselves, and have it engrafted in our hearts – from our hearts, we can speak life, love, and forgiveness. From our hearts, we can give love, comfort, and songs of praise. From our hearts we can speak and show a "wealth" of things that build others up, that exhibit Christ, that encourage ourselves, that can be the very light in someone's darkness.

Reflect over the wealth in your life. It's far more difficult to gain wings with "broke" faith. Get right church. GET right!

Peace and Blessings

Psalm 50

Let's talk about faith, loyalty, and complete trust in God. Do you have TRUE faith?

Living in this world exposes us to many sinful ways but we must be strong and wise enough to turn from those things and walk a straight and narrow path. Just because you don't indulge in the "bigger" or "major" sins does not exclude you from SIN. We must begin to live according to God's Will for our lives and rely on our faith, our loyalty, and our complete trust in God to direct our daily lives. When you wake up, thank God and pray for guidance to

get your day started. On the drive to work, thank God and pray for traveling mercies. At work, encourage someone, thank God and pray for the words you need to say. See how that works, God in everything!

NEXT, trust that all your prayer and communication with God is acknowledged. Lean not on your own understanding, but that of our wise God. Call on Him for everything, exhibit your loyalty, read His Word, communicate with Him, live according to His Word, be free from sin and encourage yourself and others. Keep God close always and never let your burdens get you down. You know the rest, Hallelujah anyhow!

Peace and Blessings

Psalm 51

When we have sinned or done wrong, we may hold some guilt regarding that sin or wrongdoing. In an effort to shed off that guilt, we must confess and repent. If we are bold enough to sin, we should be strong and bold enough to confess our sin. Once we have confessed, we must be even stronger to repent. TURN AWAY from sin, not merely tell God "I won't do it again," but really make an effort to turn away from that very sin as to no repeat it or go back to it.

When we have confessed and repented, then ask God for forgiveness. God is willing to wipe our slate clean when we have taken the steps to recognize our wrongdoing, confessed with our mouths, and repent those ways. There is nothing too hard for God, so stop trying to do things in your own strength. Stop dabbling in the wrong things and expecting God to fix it right away. Learn to stand firm on His Word and say NO TO SIN. Take ownership of your life and the way you live. Pray before making any decisions or actions. Change things about yourself that will promote healthier and less sinful living, carry your cross, love with your whole heart, and thank God for everything!

When God forgives us, He restores us. (*Repost from Psalm 32*).

Peace and Blessings

Psalm 52-53

Olive trees are some of the oldest existing trees. They are usually planted close to streams or bodies of water. Olive trees have been known to live for 200 to 2,000 years and are fruitful trees. As trees are out in the elements they are more susceptible to wear and tear, the threat of being chopped down, may dry up from the lack of water, or may not produce fruit. Olive trees seem to be destroyed when they are not planted close to water or chopped down by man.

The olive tree produces the fruit we call olive. Olives have some health and nutritional benefits and are symbolic in nature. Olives or olive leaves are known to represent peace, wisdom, glory, fertility, power, and purity.

As we have been enlightened about the olive tree, shouldn't we try to be more like an olive tree? If we are planted in God's Word, always close and drinking from the Living Water – our very being is thriving to be more fruitful. Fruitful in the way we walk, fruitful in the way we talk, and fruitful within our spiritual connect. In our fruitfulness, our thriving will begin to exhibit peace because we know God; wisdom because we read God's Word, glory because He gives us brand new mercy and grace every day, fertility because we can birth new beginnings and repent our sins, power because there is strength and victory when we accepted

Christ, and purity because we believe Jesus can wash as white as snow.

As followers of Jesus, we are susceptible to trials and tribulations, the threat of falling short, separation from God, and not demonstrating what we know about the Good News. However, when we stand firm in God's Word and withstand the wear and tear of this world, we can continue to grow strong and fruitful. Are you thriving as an olive tree?

Peace and Blessings

Psalm 54

Whenever, whatever we go through or experience, God has His loving hand on us. There should never be a day we can go without Him. Seek God daily!

Peace and Blessings

Psalm 55

"Friend". Scripture tells us to be very careful of who we choose as a "friend". A true friend will be loyal and closer than a brother and when the relationship can withstand that special bond throughout the good and bad times, you have found a friend in your brethren. The loyalty of this friend will exhibit a true heart, reliability, dependability, and trustworthiness.

Regarding these characteristics, a friendship can withstand trials, oppositions, and egotistical personalities. Furthermore, the friendship will be accepting of constructive criticism and new ideas or ways. As scripture tells us, iron sharpens iron, friends can build each other up, refine thoughts, give clarity to situations, or give insight. This is also why the Bible tells us to surround ourselves with like-minded Christians.

Debating, arguing, quarreling, not agreeing, whatever you want to call it, is not of God. God does not do confusion. If there is an issue at hand, learn to keep a calm spirit, become an active listener; find a more effective way of communicating what you want or need to say. If you disagree, get proof. If you are unable to provide proof, make an effort to find out for YOURSELF what's really in the pudding. Furthermore, constant, loud nagging is irritating and usually provides no resolution. PATIENCE WORKETH FAITH.

Knowing that God is in your heart is sufficient enough to step away from the chaos and let God and His Word cover the situation. If you have a point to prove, it can be done in love and kindness. When you approach it in a negative aspect, you have already been defeated.

Philippians 2:5 tells us to let the mind (thoughts) be in you, which is also in Christ Jesus; and Philippians 4:8 states whatsoever things are true, honest, just, pure, lovely, of good reputation, any virtue, any praise, to think on these things.

Therefore, if your thoughts are not of the stated characteristics, those very thoughts may bring strife, damnation, sin, grief, and other negative outcomes.

As we mature in our walk, our Bible reading and studying will assist in renewing our mind or thoughts. Romans 12:2 – be ye transformed by the renewing of your mind – we must change the old way we used to think, we must step out on faith as to not be conformed to the old ways or the ways of the world, but to prove what is good, acceptable, perfect, and the Will of God (Romans 12:2). We must recognize the difference between the spirit and the flesh, that the flesh may not rise but allow the spirit to move within that we may be the light or live in the manner that is conducive to God's Will. God has given us all that we need to obey and honor Him; it's our responsibility to nourish the Spirit that we may strive to be on one accord with the Word – our instructions for LIFE. Through His Word, we learn to renew our minds, no longer will those negative, pessimistic thoughts override what is engrafted into our hearts.

The time is NOW. Accept Christ into your heart, give Him room to work in you, speak death into those old fleshly ways, come boldly before the throne, as you are one of God's children and the victory is yours.

We know that the battle here on earth is won, but until we get to heaven, we must continue to do the works of God. Through His Word and obedience, you no longer see the man in the mirror, you will see Jesus, just as God does.

Peace and Blessings

Psalm 56

Trust can be described as a firm belief or strength regarding the relationship of a person or situation. We learn trust through responsibility, bonding, and risk-taking. In life, our parents taught us the significance of knowing God, how to budget money, and how to take care of ourselves. These responsibilities have built "trust" and what we have learned and how we relate to different aspects. We create relationships where we grow close to others and share intimate information and time spent – and over a period of time, we begin to trust or get comfortable with the other in the relationship. As a risk-taker, when we believe something, we are not afraid to face issues or tasks head-on because we have faith in God's Will for the outcome, and faith builds trust.

Collectively, trust describes how we should be with God. He has given us responsibility to learn lessons from His Word and live according to His Word. We must communicate with Him every day to build a relationship or bond that draws us closer to Him. We must have faith that all we do in our decision-making and actions are lined up with the Will of God and when we are, we are able to face risks or issues head-on because we TRUST what we have learned from His Word and know He would never leave nor forsake us.

Examine your heart today. Do you have trust issues? Go to God and ask Him to give you clarity. Ask Him to show you how to trust in His Word. Learn your responsibility in your spiritual walk, bond with God in His Word so that you become familiar and equipped with scripture for battle. Get grounded in the Word so that when it's time to step out on faith, you know that you can rely on God to see you through. Find trust in the Lord, then everything else will fall into place.

Peace and Blessings

Psalm 57-58

Who but God can comfort you in your time of need? Who but God prevails justice over the enemy? Who but God strengthens you when you're weak? Who but God supplies all your needs? Who but God knows everything about you from the top of your head to the bottom of your feet? Who but God knows your every thought and motive? Who but God loves you more than your parents? Who but God will never leave you nor forsake you? But God! God's mercy and grace is everlasting; God's love is surrounding; God – Great – God!

Giving honor and glory to His name, because there is no other like Him, He has turned my dark to light, I am grateful that I was chosen. Lord, hear my prayer. Thank you! You are an awesome wonder – I sing praises to Your Name! I am humbled before you! Can somebody say FAVOR!

Peace and Blessings

Psalm 59

Today is the day that the Lord has made, let us rejoice and be glad in it. These words are familiar, but are you living it? Tests and trials come daily. Expect them. The key is to know what battle you're fighting and how to fight it. So, if today poses any test or trials, know that it is a SPIRITUAL BATTLE, and we fight with THE WORD. God will never put much more on us than we can bare, so today is the day that we change our attitude, communicate with God, and build a strong relationship with Him. Know that He is the head and first in all decisions and in what we do. This is the day, when we are no longer harassed with those things that vex us in this worldliness of the day. A day when we think of God, of redemption, of hope, and of Heaven. When we think on these things, it strengthens, refreshes, and consoles the heart from burden and sorrow; it lifts the soul to joyous state of being where worrisome toll and sorrow shall be no more.

Read your Word, be encouraged, and fight any and all battles with His Word!

Peace and Blessings

Psalm 60-62

When things seem out of control or when you feel surrounded by drama or the enemy, you must remember to rely totally on God. Nothing delights God more than when we work towards His mark. We must believe and have strong enough faith to persevere through circumstances that may come up against us. We must learn to LISTEN, then make appropriate choices to move forward. We must learn to apply the Word to any situation, then carry out the victory that God told us was won. We must trust in God and know in our hearts that what He said is already done. The true point is that we must keep God first in everything we say and do.

Peace and Blessings

Psalm 63-65

The way that we behave and communicate deals with internal matters. The way we think, speak, react, interact, and abide is all controlled through the physiology of our bodies. Our bodies learn and grow from what we feed it and do for it. When we feed our bodies the nourishing Word of God, our thoughts, communication, behaviors, and obedience begin to reflect the Living Word.

We cannot see impulses of information flowing from nerve to nerve throughout our bodies that cause an outcome (speaking, behavior, etc.); therefore, we must recognize that the way we feed our internal selves is by the Word which provides the love and wisdom of God. God influences our spirit to thirst for Him. We will desire more and more once we have discovered God's greatness. His Word is more than enough.

"One who turns away his ear from hearing the law, even his prayer is an abomination." Do you need a little bit more of the basics? God detests prayers from the one who ignores the law (His Word). Your communication may be on block if you're acting like you don't know. Remember, you're responsible for what you know, so don't get frustrated when you feel your prayers are in limbo. Go to our Father right. You can't hide anything from Him anyway.

Do some meditation, soul search, call on God, get right, START,

MAKE AN EFFORT, ACTION, MOVE, DO IT FOR REAL. Make the change in your life that line up with God's Word, you know what they are.

Peace and Blessings

Psalm 66-67

When we are battling decisions, hurting, or have confusion, we can go to God in prayer. We can even get intimate with Him and cry out in our own personal closet. In our closet, we confess, snot, cry, pour out emotions, speak life, seek comfort, and when God sees fit, we get delivered. Delivered from the things that had us bound, upset us, off track, wavering, or what has separated us from the love of God.

God honors His relationships with His children and will be in the midst when we call on Him. When God has allowed us to come through a battle, we must let others know the victory that was won. We must give God His props when He brings us through, when He allows the desires of our heart, when He makes changes for the better, when He has given us the answer to our prayers, and when

He allows us to see things come to pass. These things are testimonies. A testimony is evidence or truth from a witness and when we have testimonies, we can encourage someone else or let them see how God works. We can provide insight into a battle someone is going through or a battle that we may have already been through and were victorious in the end. We are not to be ashamed or embarrassed, but willing to speak boldly about our experiences and give God the glory for the outcomes.

With God, we can be delivered from anything, and when we are delivered, we should let others know how great God is through our testimonies.

Peace and Blessings

Psalm 68-69

When dealing with everyday situations, we must decide what's spiritually best for ourselves as well as what it is that we're experiencing and if it's spiritually sound. We must familiarize or recognize the things (impurities) that could draw us from our goal, could taint our thoughts, could lead to bad decisions, harmful acts, hurtful language, or cause a stumble in our spiritual walk.

In the Old Testament when people took sacrifices to the altar, God said to bring CLEAN (without blemish) sacrifices unto Him. In Romans 12:1, we are to offer our bodies as a living sacrifice, holy and acceptable unto God, which is our REASONABLE service. Therefore, as believers and doers of the Word, we should cleanse ourselves of all impurities so that we may reasonably serve God. This cleansing will also deter us from being sucked into sin. What impurities need to be cleansed? Those things you claim - "I'll stop smoking next month," "I am too busy to read and pray every day," or claiming you trust God, but keep trying to make things happen in your own strength. See, these things are not pure – they are clouds of dust that can sometimes make our goal or what is expected fuzzy to see – the focus becomes unfocused – the focus should be your reasonable service to God, communicating with Him, reading and studying His Word, and living Christ-like.

The blood of Jesus has cleansed us white as snow, but yet we track through the mud and the snow becomes dirty. Cleansing impurities allows us to avoid the mud and radiate or let our light shine. When we are cleansed and shining, the intense reflection will exhibit purity.

Another thing - the mouthpiece. We all know there is life and death in the tongue, but how much do we really take that to heart?

We can speak damnation or life into situations, including ourselves. Scripture tells us to speak those things as though they are (Romans 4:17), not lie, but speak optimistically towards situations, desires, and concerns, in prayer. Gossiping, bad mouthing, claiming to know it all, arguing, and the use of offensive sayings or gestures all taint or hurt one's self or others. Be slow to speak until you have thoroughly sifted through your thoughts that ultimately influence your speech.

Are you trusting? What is trust? I define trust as being able to rely on, having faith, or belief in. I find that I have become more trusting and trustworthy as I mature in my spirituality. Things that used to make me mad, disappointed, not trusting, or outright ticked off, no longer have me bound. I am led by what I believe in the Word and as I become equipped with God's Wisdom, I can decipher the characteristics that exhibit trustworthiness in myself as well as others. Satan gets no glory with me; however, I do know he is very cunning, and he asks permission all the time to get at me. So I know that he will play tricks with "trust," but be assured that I am covered. God said he would never leave nor forsake me, so I use careful decision-making and consideration to what or who I trust.

I strive to offer hope and accountability to others that they may find a friend in me and aspire to reflect Christ-likeness. Through it all, the good and the bad, and like God – I strive to never leave or forsake another, (in conversation or situation) that could lead to damnation.

Interaction with others can influence, taint, encourage, damage, reconcile, or separate people. How we conduct our behavior and conversation speak volumes of our personalities and respect we have for ourselves and others. Matthew 7:17 tells us to do unto others as you will have them do to you. You know how you want to be treated or spoken to, reciprocate the same. No good comes from evil, and I'll leave it at that.

Peace and Blessings

Psalm 70-72

God wants His people to get along and interact with each other as needed. As believers we are to recognize when others are in need of help, spiritually or physically. Our words should be encouraging or leading to a more optimistic outcome. We must have discernment to identify when our brother or sister is in need and allow God to use us however is fit for the situation. The key is to be in tune with our discernment and let the spirit move. When we allow the spirit to move in us and not address situations or conversations out of our flesh, God will get the glory

and the one in need will have encouragement to keep pressing.

Philippians 4:19 tells us that God will supply all of our needs, and indeed He will. God also use His people - us, to carry out some of the actions needed to help others. When we operate in God's Will, He will allow the unthinkable. We may never understand the full joy of someone who is down and out, but they were grateful because we were able to give them $20, good advice, a ride to work, food for the night, a place to lay their head, or even just a hug. Our minds must be like Christ, full of compassion and ready to serve. Know that God smiles upon obedience, and He will reward those who follow His Word in His Way!

We complain all the time about what we go through. At some point, we call on God in prayer. However, scripture tells us to pray, unceasingly. I Thessalonians 5:17 and James 5:16 tells us that the effectual fervent prayer of the righteous avails much. Therefore, if we pray all the time, it would become effective and will reveal much. If we continue to go against God's Word in our actions, heart, or conversations, and do not pray as instructed, God will have a deaf ear to our prayers. Proverbs 28:9; Isaiah 59:2 states, "But your iniquities have made a separation between you and your God, and your sins have hidden His face from you so that He does not hear." Proverbs 15:29 states, "The Lord is far from the wicked, but He hears the prayer of the righteous." Therefore, we must pray and pray some more; praying must be part of our daily breathing or risk God not hearing our prayers.

When we have sinned, done wrong, or made a mistake, for the most part we like to keep it concealed or covered up. Well, our God is omniscient, and He knows all, so you are not hiding anything from Him. If God is the only one who can judge you, why would you hide something from those who cannot put you in a heaven or hell?

Admitting or confessing sins, wrongs, or mistakes will set you free. You will no longer be bound to a burden that you selfishly claim. When you cover up sin, wrongs, or mistakes, you are claiming and hoarding it. When you admit or confess, you are

allowing correction to come about and mature from the lesson learned. We cannot be so prideful that we cannot be truthful with others, let alone ourselves. No one is perfect, but the Creator, and the Creator has given us opportunities to become more like Him and to create a new man within us that we may strive to live holy and righteous. Although we fall short, God gives brand new mercies every day. This is not a free ticket to continue to do what you do, but to recognize and grow through the situation, knowing that honesty, rebuking, and repenting from sin is a charge from God. Furthermore, acknowledging our wrongs or mistakes helps us to forgive ourselves and what we have done.

God knows YOU and everything about YOU. He asked that you know Him through His Word and prayer. This is not a charge, but a choice, God has given us a choice.

Will you be about your Father's business or do you choose the world?

Peace and Blessings

Psalm 73

We must learn to level out the scales of good and bad; right from wrong; and righteous and wicked. We should have already begun to veer from the negativity in our lives that draw us to the ways that are not of God. We should be focusing on how to get right, stay right, and reveal God's marvelous being as the only way to a prosperous, yet eternal life. By no means should we think that living for God will be easy. Was it for Christ? We must begin to fight the battle through our words and behaviors that are influenced by the Living Word which is also our daily life's guide. I cannot express enough how important it is to know God, His word, and to walk the walk. We use excuses after excuses about why we have not done certain things in life, starting with the small things that eventually lead to a compilation of things. We must begin to speak life – God's Word, into our own lives and others. We must STOP and evaluate each situation we deal with that weigh on our minds, that influence our behaviors, and begin to use what we know about God and His Word

to get on one accord with Him and how He wants us to live. We must begin to stand firm under pressure, listen before answering, be accepting to HONESTY, and ACTUALLY MAKE EFFORTS.

We must feed on the Word day and night, let the Word be manifested through us, learn to fast and pray, and draw closer to God. The more we read His Word, the more we become familiar with what is expected of us and the stronger we become in our thoughts, communication, and behaviors. God knows our hearts. Do you know His?

Our God is so awesome, He does not force us to do anything, but He gives us a choice; we can live abundantly or carelessly. When we do not accept divine guidance, that is the guidance of God, we run wild, but if we are accepting and obey the Word, we can live in joy.

Developing a true relationship with God means that we have action that needs to be taken, not once or twice, but all the days of our lives, no breaks, no excuses, He should be first and foremost in everything we do or say. He should be the author and the finisher of any situation we are in. He should be the head of our lives, calling on Him for all that we need. If He is not, it's past time to get it right.

Father God, I am praying that my brothers and sisters begin to look like You with a new meaning, with the seriousness of Your call on our lives, that we may shun our old ways and begin to let our spirit man shine, that our actions in words begin to reflect that of You, that the things we put off are now on task, that the excuses we use are no longer in our thoughts, that the struggles we have are under our feet, that You God get the glory out of every move we make and every word we say, have us to know You better, have us to get on one accord, have us to be an encouragement of Your Word for others, have us to live according to Your Word that we may gain the ultimate prize, which is eternal life with You. I praise You God and give you all of the glory. I pray for forgiveness for all of our sins, that we may become right with You and continue on this straight and narrow path that seems to be a struggle at times; help us Lord to trust and call on You when we feel we have nowhere else to turn. You said You would never leave or forsake us, and we stay in firm

knowing that. Giving You all of the praise and honor, thank You Jesus for your saving grace, thank You Jesus for taking it all when we were so undeserving, thank You Jesus for every test and trial that draws us closer to You, thank You Jesus for just being the awesome example for our lives. Bless us as You see fit, we ask all of these things in Your precious name. Amen!

Peace and Blessings

Psalm 74-77

So many times we try to handle things in our own strength, but our strength is not always sufficient like Jesus, we must learn to PRAY and GIVE our weariness and burdens over to Him (we give it over by reading and knowing His Word and applying the Word to our lives and life situations). We must learn that even when we give things over to Him that we must be patient and watch how He unfolds the outcome. We must stop complaining and wanting a microwave minute outcome. If you have gotten off track with your relationship with God and your reading is at a standstill, how do you think God feels when you come begging for answers and outcomes from Him?

We must do our part in the relationship and stop acting like we have not fallen short. Communicate with God on a daily basis, read your Word and let it seep into your soul, repent your old ways and let the new man grow. You are no longer on breast milk but table food. Stand firm on what you believe in and do not let the wiles of this world get you down, instead be a soldier in God's army. For God, so loved the world that He gave His only begotten Son (could you?). Respect who is all powerful, almighty, all giving, omnipresent, and all you can ask or think. No more pity parties, no more complaining, and no more trying in your own strength. Give God what He is due...your attention, time, and obedience.

Peace and Blessings

Psalm 78-80

Biblical history has shown that ups and downs of human relationships and interactions with God occur.

However, God devised a plan of His children for His own liking. When we, God's children, make choices that are not of His nature, trouble is among us. We must use our godly discretion in things, not one or some, but all things! We become leaders or soldiers for Christ through our actions and words, our light will shine when God has been put first.

The quality of one's life draws attention. Attention to what? To one's trustworthiness, patience, kindness, dedication, and honesty. We cannot lead others to Christ when we are not modeling the goodness of Christ and all that He is. He is marvelous, all powerful, almighty, sovereign, and supreme. Every ounce of steam we have in us should be used to glorify our God. We learn, attain, and gain our Christ-likeness from communion with Him, prayer, fellowship with like-minded, and living according to His Word. Self-evaluate. Are you missing any attribute that could stunt your relationship with Jesus? Are you the leader God has called you to be?

It's time, get right and don't let the encounters of this world, test, or trials snuff out your light!

Peace and Blessings

Psalm 81-82

Despite the things we have done, God has provided a way in which we can reflect and make light of our shortcomings. When we have veered away from doing right, God allows us to repent. Repenting is not a way out, but a manner of reflection. When we repent, we must recognize the wrongdoing, confess the wrongdoing, then turn from the wrongdoing as to not go back or repeat the wrongdoing. Once we have repented, we must build our strength in the Lord. We begin to set our sights on Christ-like attributes and strive to be more like Christ. We must learn to be avid readers of the Word and apply the Word to our daily life.

We must learn how to talk to and treat others; even when others have been wrong or undeserving. We must speak life into all situations we are a part of. Would Jesus leave you hanging? To answer that. No. So we must learn how to evaluate every snare, every stripe, every issue, and every devil

that think you are easy prey. Know who you are in Christ and make a stand and demand sin and drama out of your life. Live for Christ, just as He died for us.

Peace and Blessings

Psalm 83-84

Our God is an awesome God; He reigns from Heaven above with wisdom, power, and love; our God is an awesome God.

During our spiritual walk, we must remember to keep God first and rely on Him for wisdom; wisdom to decipher right from wrong, wisdom to speak against those things that may come against us, wisdom that express the endurance to press through any situation or circumstance. We can express power through the words that we speak. We can speak life into wilting situations, we can speak life to an achy heart, and we can speak life to the weary.

We can express love through the sharing of the Word, love by praying and caring for each other, love through a single hug, love through the reading of the Word, and love by humbling ourselves and abiding by God's calling to His people.

Collectively, we experience God's awesomeness when we seek our wisdom from God and apply it to our everyday living. We are powerful when we speak God's Word to any and every situation, trial, or test, we share love when we have put God first and withstand the wiles of this world.

During your day, conversations, and interactions remember that God's wisdom, power, and love makes for an alliance that encourages spiritual growth, communion with righteousness, and adoration from God.

Peace and Blessings

Psalm 85-86

Sometimes we slip into a rut that causes us to be down and out or out of tune. When we are at a low point; we can call on God to revive us. God can restore our very being. When we pray, He hears us. When we read, He prepares us. When we seek wisdom, He provides for us, and when we are obedient, He allows our walk to become stronger.

No matter the situation, God can, God will, and God is. Through it all seek the most high and allow God to direct your path. Never give into what has you bound. When it's time to let go of our problems or issues, release them to God and He will work it out. When it's time to cleanse your mind and soul, learn to fast and release (cry). When you feel lost or overwhelmed, call on Jesus. When you think nothing else could go wrong and it does, know that God would never leave or forsake you. We serve a mighty God and He has equipped us to survive and conquer all. Muster up, woman up, man up, move forward in His word, for we are victorious and the battle is won.

We are God's children. We must represent Him in our walk, talk, and actions. We must stand bold before our situations and put out fires with the Living Water. God is so worthy! Seek Him and see for yourself. He is all we ever need.

Peace and Blessings

Psalm 87-88

As believers in Christ Jesus, we must congregate together or be among like-minded. Together, we can share in the love, grace, and mercy that God has shown us through our daily lives and those close to us. Godly and supportive friendships provide a lifestyle of caring, giving, and receiving to include wisdom and edification that builds love and commitment. Words of kindness, love, and wisdom are shared in this bond – a meeting of the mind –challenging and stimulating – living in good company as opposed to corrupt company. Two or more are stronger than one – surround yourself with godly friends – they have your best interest at heart – iron sharpens iron. He who walks with wise men will be wise.

When we feel we are at our lowest, the encouragement from another believer can be the very thing that triggers one's spirit to seek God. Sometimes we feel so low we don't know how to pray or get to God. God seems far away when the mind and the heart are heavy, but lo and behold, God is here. God will never leave or forsake us; however, God will allow us to go through.

He will allow us to learn from our tests and trials. He will allow us to use His Word to fight any battle, and He will allow us to come unto Him for comfort and peace. We will never go through anything that God can't bring us through. Stay strong, pray unceasingly, equip yourself for battle, keep pressing for the mark, don't find yourself lost, because God has your back. Consult with God. He knows you better than you know yourself.

Peace and Blessings

Psalm 89

God is completely reliable! Reliable to keep His Word, reliable to see you through any situation, reliable to answer prayers, reliable to protect you, and reliable to save you. He is completely reliable. God's deity is over all and conquers all. To allow His power to flow through us; we must read His Word, study His Word, role play His Word, and pray for the fruition of His Word. We can receive God's promises when we exhibit obedience and loyalty. Just as God promised David that his descendants would reign forever,

God has promised blessing for those who keep His Word. We have been commissioned to follow and do the greater works of God's Word. We must be strong enough to tread through the wilderness. We must be wise in decision-making and give God glory in every aspect of our being. Live life for God, live life that we should receive eternal life. Do not slumber, rely on the strength that God supplies and live in His Word for the rest of the days of our lives.

Peace and Blessings

Psalm 90-91

Many times we get caught up in our daily lives and some days we have not given God His due praise. Times of trouble, sadness, illness, and even laziness all seem to weigh heavy in our lives. During these times, we sometimes find ourselves trying to "figure" it out and herein lies the problem. When we are going through times of trouble, sadness, illness, or being lazy, we must seek the only one who can help us – God. God is our refuge, our fortress, and He can give us relief to any issue or situation. We must learn to lean on God, communicate with God, GO TO GOD; we must not and cannot wait on what "we" think, but "seek" wisdom and guidance from God. When you're in trouble, pray that God gives you wisdom and protection. When you're sad, pray that God gives you comfort and understanding. When you're sick, pray that God will heal you. When you're lazy, pray that God will give you energy to prosper. There is nothing our God can't do, and He answers prayers! Build your relationship with God and allow Him to direct your path in all things.

Peace and Blessings

Psalm 92-94

What is the status of your personality health? Is your personality strong and vibrant or is it weak and spiteful? Do you use good judgment? Are you aware of situations and things going on around you? Do you show attention to only what you desire? Are you on the right track and press to stay there? When we use good judgment, we are using Christ-like attributes, we activate a collective perception of experiences and knowledge that relies on sound reasoning. Good judgment does not insinuate that the way you would do something or the way you think is always right. Good judgment means that you have weighed the options that are connected to what is being decided over and then going with the best choice. In the event that the judgment is not pleasant, we must learn to make these unpleasant judgments in love.

Awareness is also part of good judgment. We must be aware of things that are going on in our homes, jobs, communities, government, schools, and other vital areas. When we are aware of these things, we are enlightened on what we need to pray about, and we gain knowledge. This very knowledge can help us make good judgment on issues that we are not involved in but can begin to express ourselves in helpful ways once we understand what is going on. We also gain awareness when we pay attention to issues or situations that we normally do not partake in or that we have not been introduced to. Our attention

brings consciousness and concentration; giving attention leads to awareness, that ultimately assists in good judgment. Finally, when we have linked attention, awareness, and good judgment, we can find it less difficult to stay on the right track. In order to stay on the right track to God, we must use careful discretion and judgment or decisions that we make. Our judgment and decisions must be lined up with God, if not, we will experience unnecessary stumbles.

We go through test and trials to grow our faith and become mature in God's Word. We must learn to endure and press through the hard times in life that we may experience. Just as fire tests silver and gold, we can come out purified when we pass a test or press through trials. And again, this is where our attention, awareness, and good judgment play a part in how we choose to keep striving in our walk with God or we stumble, get back up and try it again. Don't settle for do overs, strive to get it right the first time. Let your personality be that of Christ-likeness. If you experience the same type of situations or drama over and over again and they are not for the building of your spirituality or the kingdom, then reevaluate what you can improve – your attention span, your awareness, or the logical or reasonable judgment that you make. Make some changes in your personality in how you communicate or interact and watch the light in you become a little more brighter.

Peace and Blessings

Psalm 95-96

We have discussed prayer, trials, tests, self-awareness, and how to proceed in this world we live in. We have prayed, we have endured tests and trials, we have made positive changes in our spiritual walk, and we have made good decisions to walk in faith. Because of this, we have reason to give God His due praise! God has created us, the world, and the fullness thereof. If God has created everything, including the things we love, want, and desire, shouldn't we give God His props? Songs, shouts, and gratitude should erupt from our very being because God has allowed us to live. Not only has He

allowed us to live, especially when we have sinned, God has given us knowledge and strength to remain victorious in this corrupt world. Do not slumber when times seem to be going well, sing praises unto God, worship and adore Him, give God your attention; God is grateful to feel the love He has so graciously shown us.

Father God, we thank You once again that we are able to wake another day that we may serve You. I pray that we are able to indulge in Your Word, and it becomes the daily instructions for our lives, that we may do the greater work that You have called us to do, that we may be righteous in Your eyes. We stand firm knowing that You are our Creator and that You know all, so we ask that You condition our hearts to veer from wickedness and the trials of this world, that we may be strong contenders in this spiritual battle. I pray for strength and understanding for all who are coming unto You, give them a mind and heart to want more of You. You are amazing, You are awesome, and You are almighty. We thank You Lord, we give You all of the praise and honor. We lift Your name on high. Bless us as only You can, and we ask all this in Your precious son's name. Amen!

Peace and Blessings

Psalm 97-100

Today's reading reminds us that worship and praise is a vital piece in our relationship with God. God is our Creator and deserves our worship and highest praise. Through the good or the bad, ups or downs - God reigns. God's majesty and goodness alone is a reason for us to worship and praise Him. Even more specific we can reflect on how God has brought us through storms; healed sickness, provided for our needs, never leaves nor forsakes; protects us; and provides a piece of mind. We could go on and on testifying about what God has done. We must now continually do our part, worship and praise Him. Just as we pray over ourselves, our lives, the desires of our hearts, and find joy in our relationship with God, God wants that joy reciprocated back to Him. Every day we should be giving God His due worship and praise.

Father God, I am praying that we begin to look to You with new meaning, with the seriousness of Your call on our lives, that we may shun our old ways and begin to let our spirit man shine. Let our actions and words begin to reflect that of You, and the things we put off are now on task, that the excuses we use are no longer excuses, that the struggles we have are under our feet, and that You God get the glory out of every move we make and every word we say.

Have us to know You better, have us to get on one accord, have us to be an encouragement of Your Word for others, have us to live according to Your Word that we may gain the ultimate prize, which is eternal life with You, and for this, WE praise You God and give you all of the glory! I pray for forgiveness for all of our sins, that we may become right with You and continue on this straight and narrow path that seems to be a struggle at times. Help us Lord to trust and call on You when we feel we have nowhere else to turn. You said you would never leave us nor forsake us, and we stand firm knowing that. We give You all the praise and honor. Thank You Jesus for Your saving grace. Thank You Jesus for taking it all when we were so undeserving. Thank You Jesus for every test and trial that draw us closer to You. Thank You Jesus for being an awesome example for our lives. Bless us as You see fit. We ask all of these things in Your precious name. Amen!

Peace and Blessings

Psalm 101-102

Trust can be described as a firm belief or strength regarding the relationship of a person or situation. We learned trust through responsibility, bonding, and risk-taking. In life, our parents taught us the significance of knowing God, how to budget money, and how to take care of ourselves – these responsibilities have built "trust" and what we have learned and how we relate to different aspects of our lives.

We create relationships where we grow close to others and share intimate information and time spent, and over time, we begin to trust or get comfortable with others in the relationship or bond. As a risk-taker – when we believe something, we are not afraid to face issues head-on because we have faith in God's Will for the outcome; and faith builds trust.

Collectively, trust describes how we should be with God. He has given us responsibility to learn lessons from His Word and live according to His Word; we must communicate with Him every day to build the relationship or bond that draws us closer to Him; we must have faith in all that we do, in our decision-making, and that our actions are lined up with the Will of God - and when we are, we are able to face trials or issues head-on because we TRUST what we have learned from His Word.

Peace and Blessings

Psalm 103-104

When we seek, we shall find, when we knock, He will answer, when we ask, we shall receive. God has been so good to US that there should never be a day that goes by that we don't recognize and

THANK God.

Peace and Blessings

Psalm 105

History reveals past events and lessons to be learned. The history of God's children involved promises and disobedience. God made promises with Abraham, Isaac, Jacob, and for their descendants. During this time, people became impatient and began to doubt and disobey God in His Word. This disobedience led to punishment and wrath, however, God still was true to His promises. What does this teach us?

Biblical history teaches and serves as a guide of what to do and what not to do. Becoming familiar with Bible history provides for wisdom that can be reflected to make decisions or provide clarity. Overall, we must come to know our Bible history, learn God's decrees, and line up accordingly.

We gain insight and lessons from both the Old and New Testaments of the Bible. The purpose is to teach people how to attain wisdom, discipline, and how to live right, just, and fair. The teachings address family life, self-control, resisting temptations, business matters, marriage, knowing God, seeking the truth, wealth, poverty, immorality, and wisdom (just to name a few). We must adhere to what the Bible can teach us and put those teachings into learned behaviors. When we have learned these teachings, our learned behaviors will exhibit strong characteristics that include wisdom, relationship building, good attitudes, hard work, and successful living.

Know our Bible history, learn what God has provided for us and discover the source, value, and benefits of godly living. God knows EVERYTHING about you, how much do you know about Him?

Peace and Blessings

Psalm 106-107

Think of all the miracles God has personally done for you: birth, personal development, salvation, specific guidance, healing, and He loves you. All too often we cloud these very things in our minds and give into the allurements of this world. We must remember to keep miracles in the forefront as to not sway from God's guidance and miracles. We must fight a never-ending battle that temps us to sway, but by God's Word, the battle is already won. We must keep the faith and allow God to direct our path. Reflect on your personal miracles and give God His praise.

Peace and Blessings

Psalm 108-109

We cannot serve God and sin. What we read, listen to, talk about, or watch is a part of our mental diet. When the mind is given garbage (sinful thoughts, negative thoughts, etc.), our minds become influenced by those very things. We must take careful consideration what we feed our minds, then we can become spiritually healthy in our thoughts. We can nurture ourselves with the goodness of God's Word and reap spiritually sound thoughts, words, and behaviors.

Peace and Blessings

Psalm 110-111

No worries! No worries because God has not given us a spirit of fear, no worries because God protects us, no worries because God will make our enemies our footstools, no worries because God tells us the victory is ours, and no worries because we are free to call on Him whenever for whatever. Praise Him for no worries. Praise Him because He loves us. Praise Him for waking us up. Praise Him for His grace and mercy. Praise Him because that is our reasonable service. Praise Him because HE LIVES! Delight in the Lord, pray unceasingly, and never let your burdens get you down!

Peace and Blessings

Psalm 112-114

112 Be of good nature, be confident, fearless, and do good deeds.

113 God gives, provides, and makes all things possible.

114 God can allow or make mountains move, part water, and turn dark to light.

We are nothing without God, and when we begin to indulge in His greatness, we can reap the fruit of living here on Earth. Take a moment and reflect on how great God is!

Peace and Blessings

Psalm 115-118

Reflect on the goodness of Jesus. Reflect on the prayers He has answered, the blessing He has bestowed, and the faithfulness He provides. If He does nothing else for us, He still is worthy of our highest praise. We must continue to put our confidence in the Lord and allow Him to direct our words and path. We must lean not on our own understanding, but allow God's unfailing love and faithfulness to consume our thoughts and being. No matter what we go through, what's going on, how we feel, or how it looks, God always gives us a reason to give Him praise. Reflect and always give God praise!

Peace and Blessings

Psalm 119

God's word is true and wonderful. Stay faithful to God and His Word no matter how bad the world becomes. Obedience to God's Word is the only way to achieve real happiness.

Keywords in today's scripture: decree, instruction, and Commandments.

For any situation, remember God's decree for guidance and instruction, follow through with God's Commandments, and keep them in your heart, for God's Commandments are deterrents for sin.

Peace and Blessings

Psalm 120-124

These chapters detail the songs of thoughts during life's journey of that time. These chapters remind us that we must seek God, carry out His commands with trust, and to be encouraged to press for right living. We give God worship and praise for victory, protection, blessings, grace, and mercy. Because of whom God is, we give Him praise!

Peace and Blessings

Psalm 125-129

These few chapters speak of God's unfailing love. He is our protector, He can free us from bondage, He is our foundation, He directs our path, He brings us out of rough times, and He restores. Who but God can comfort you in your time of need? Who but God prevails justice over the enemy? Who but God strengthens you when you are weak? Who but God can supply all your needs? Who but God knows everything about you from the top of your head to the bottom of your feet? Who but God knows you're every thought and motive? Who but God loves you more than your parents? Who but God will never leave you or forsake you? But God! God's mercy and grace is everlasting; God – Great – God!

We give honor and glory to His name, no other like Him, He has turned our dark to light, we are grateful that we were chosen. Lord, hear our prayer, Thank You! You are an awesome wonder, and we sing praises to Your name! We are humbled before You! (Repost from Psalm 57-58).

Peace and Blessings

Psalm 130-134

Every day we wake, God employs new mercies and grace. God also forgives us for our sins but, we must confess those sins in order for them to be forgiven. Reflect over your daily actions and words. Ask God for forgiveness for anything that is not of Him or His Word. Begin to recognize the things that you need to avoid as to not repeat the same sin. God is our true help and provider; and keeping a clean slate with Him to always allow prosperous living. Seek God in all things and pray for forgiveness. When we have prayed, we can exhibit our trust in God by turning away from sin and know in our hearts that God has forgiven us, and that He will continue to love and guide us.

We can live in contentment because of what God says in His Word, who He is, and because God is almighty and forgiving. We must honor God in our walk, talk, and every interaction. We must show ourselves to be Christ-like, not be weary, and lead others to our Heavenly Father. We must hold fast to our beliefs and trust in God, build our character and relationships accordingly, and allow the Word of God to manifest itself through our daily lives. Collectively, we can live a joyous life with God's blessings when we pray, forgive, seek Him in all things, trust in Him, honor Him, and encourage others.

Question: are you living a joyous and blessed life or that of turmoil and sin?

Peace and Blessings

Psalm 135-138

Chapter 135 reiterate that we must praise God for who He is and His greatness.

Chapter 136 reminds us of God's great love and that His love

endures forever. Chapter 137 reminds us that we will have times of weeping, but we must overcome our weeping and sing praises unto God. For any situation we find as a struggle, it will pass. Chapter 138 reminds us that God will work out every aspect of our lives and we must continue to give Him praises of thanksgiving for all He has done for us.

Give God His praise; allow Him to wholeheartedly love you; endure and grow from times of weeping; and continually thank God.

Peace and Blessings

Psalm 139-143

How much do you really want God in your life? Allowing God in our lives mean we must surrender to God and to stop trying to operate in our own strength. We must begin to look to God who is almighty and all-powerful. The things we do in life are nothing if we don't have God in it. We must recognize and begin to trust God in all that we do and say. We must stand firm on what we know and learn about God not to be bamboozled by any wind of doctrine, action, or misinterpretation. We are to be heavyweights in God, not lightweights that can be easily knocked down. Seek God with your heart and confess with your mouth, He is Lord. Try him and you will see, nothing is as good or satisfying as our God!

Peace and Blessings

Psalm 144-145

As God is our protector, provider, go to, and giver of blessings, we must continually worship and praise Him for who He is and all He does for us individually and collectively. We can call on God every day for anything. We must pray with a focus. A focus that encompasses our families, church, friends, neighbors, acquaintances, situations, issues, health, mindset, and who God is in our lives. Be diligent in prayer and faith so that no weapon shall prosper; the enemy is not victorious; and that you may grow in Christ.

Spend time with the Lord through reading and studying His Word, through prayer, through worship,

in your secret closet, and in your heart. Show God your appreciation and adoration towards Him, for He has done great things for us and things that we could never fathom. Fear the Lord and praise Him forever. He will protect who He loves and grant desires and blessings to those who are obedient.

Peace and Blessings

Psalm 146-150

The last few chapters in the Book of Psalms repeat the very action we should do daily...Praise the Lord! The Book of Psalms parallels our spiritual journey through life. It begins by presenting us with two roads: the road to life and the road to death. If we choose God's road to life, we still face both blessings and troubles, joy and grief, and success and obstacles. Through it all God will be by our side, guiding, encouraging, comforting, and caring. And for this, we give Him praise!

Peace and Blessings

2
Walking Through Proverbs

As children of God, we get many of our teachings from the book of Proverbs. The purpose of Proverbs is to teach people how to attain wisdom, discipline, and how to live right, just, and fair. The teachings in Proverbs address family life, self-control, resisting temptations, business matters, marriage, knowing God, seeking the truth, wealth, poverty, immorality, and wisdom (just to name a few). A little history - Proverbs is a Hebrew word for "to rule or to govern." Therefore, God has provided us with the rules to govern our lives. We must adhere to what the Book of Proverbs can teach us and put those teachings into learned behaviors. When we have learned these teachings, our learned behaviors will exhibit strong characteristics that include wisdom, relationship building, good attitudes, hard work, and successful living.

These chapters reflect my feelings and encouragement while walking through the Book of Proverbs.

Let the Proverbs begin...

Proverbs 1

The first chapter of Proverbs is the basic instruction or advice to assist the believer in discovering God's Wisdom. The words are not just supposed to be read but instruct us to do what the scriptures are saying. We must learn to apply what the Word is saying and understand how to correlate the instruction or advice into our everyday living. Adhering to the instruction and advice of Proverbs teaches discipline, guidance, and right from wrong. Proverbs is a Hebrew word defined as "to rule or to govern." Therefore, in reading Proverbs, we are to rule or govern our words and actions according to God's Will and His Word. The difference between knowledge and wisdom is knowledge is having the facts and wisdom are APPLYING those facts to life.

Proverbs 2:6 tells us that God gives wisdom. However, we have a role in receiving that wisdom. We must earnestly seek knowledge and understanding of His Word. We must trust God and realize that the Bible reveals God's Wisdom to us. Therefore, to acquire wisdom from God, we must have a relationship with God, His Word, and a connection with His Will and His Way. We must evolve from the flesh and allow the spirit to be fed by the Word. The more the Word is in us, we have no choice but to change or transform. The Word will begin to convict us of those things that are not of God, and we will begin to comprehend God's agape love for us. Furthermore, we will begin to get the true meaning that everything that glitters isn't gold.

We are quick to judge others, shoot down what another has to say, or even proclaim to know more than what we really do, this is because of wavering faith. We must open our SPIRITUAL hearts, eyes, ears, and minds, and recognize that we all fall short of the glory of God, (but God gives us grace). When we do this, God will allow us to gain insight of Him and His Word. God's Word SHOULD be governing our lives.

Furthermore, we must heed to His Word and use Proverbs for the reason it was provided...to attain wisdom, discipline, how to conduct ourselves, and to apply God's Word in daily living. God so loved the world that He gave His only begotten Son (John 3:16). What an awesome God we have that He would give His only Son for our sins. Can you imagine giving up one of your children for everyone in the world? The charge God has given us is much easier; read and abide by His Word.

Matthew 11:30 tells us that God's yolk is easy, and the burden is light. This means that God's yolk (connection or bond) is easy. The yolk that sin imposes is heavy, and bearing it brings no rest. The yolk of false or corrupted religion is burdensome; but Christ's yolk is easy. It is not hard to bear because it is bonded in love. "My burden is light." His burden, even if it is the cross, is light, because He helps us to bear or to endure.

Fools despise wisdom and discipline (Proverbs 1:7). However, we must press on to draw ourselves closer to God and press to live according to His Word, THEN we will discover and develop the value and benefits of wisdom and discipline.

Peace and Blessings

Proverbs 2

WISDOM is an awesome gift from God. God has given us an opportunity to intimately connect with Him, not only through love, but through knowing Him. The constant process of growing in God's Wisdom involves knowing where wisdom comes from, how to decipher right from wrong, knowing that attaining God's wisdom is a lifelong journey, and that there are lessons in gaining wisdom. Job 28:12– 28 gives full detail that wisdom is a gift from God, YES!, Another gift! How do we get the gift? Read it! Yes, indeed, wisdom is gained from the reading and studying of God's Word. Reading and studying are the easy parts of attaining this gift; however, we must also practice, put into action, and DO what the Word tells us. We can read and study all day, but faith without works is dead (James 2:20). Get in tune with your spirituality, become familiar with the steps to develop consistency in communicating with God, reading and studying His Word AND carrying out the appropriate actions as seen fit by His Word. Wisdom is given so that we can rely on it and press through situations, tests, and trials. Wisdom will keep us from missing out on opportunities that God may allow; wisdom will nurture maturity; and wisdom produces optimal results.

God has given us all the gifts and tools we need to receive eternal life. We must learn to use the gifts and tools to bring glory to God and to benefit our time here on earth. Seek God and He shall direct thy path.

Peace and Blessings

Proverbs 3

Proverbs 3 reiterates loyalty, kindness, and wisdom. Our loyalty should be to the Lord. Everything we do, say, and come across, should be dealt with, said, or connected with the love of God that is in our hearts. Loyalty reflects our faithfulness, trustworthiness, commitment, and obedience to God and His Word. When we practice these characteristics, they will shine like a light, others will not have to be told, but they will recognize that you have loyalty to God.

Being kind seems easy and simple, but for some of us, it's like pulling teeth. We are quick to get an attitude when something does not go our way or if someone says something we disagree with. When we exhibit kindness, good nature, understanding, and unselfishness, we can agree to disagree. However, the agree/disagree scenario should be done in love. When we are able to decipher differences, we are more likely to keep a caring and considerate attitude and in turn, our attitudes exhibit the characteristics of a kind person.

Finally, this chapter also speaks of WISDOM (again). The repetitiveness of wisdom throughout the Book of Proverbs is a cue to how important it is to seek God and His Word for wisdom. Wisdom can bring many benefits to our everyday lives. Knowing right from wrong or how to decipher a situation or conversation will always give God glory if we are exercising the wisdom that God has graciously allowed us to obtain. Seeking wisdom through God's Word will influence how we categorize priorities and what we place value on. Therefore, it is imperative that we communicate with God to know Him for ourselves, that we may yield to His Word, attain knowledge and wisdom and live according to His Will.

Peace and Blessings

Proverbs 4

Over and over God's word is telling us to seek wisdom. Proverbs 4 is pounding into our brains and hearts that wisdom is necessary for righteous living and helps determine the outlook in which we choose to operate or interact on a daily basis.

Seeking wisdom from God will cue us to choose the correct path for our lives, the straight and narrow path that leads to eternal life or the wide and wicked path that leads to self-destruction.

Obtaining God's wisdom is also beneficial for our immediate and extended families. We can encourage our families to direct their focus to God and His Word, so that they too, will know the goodness of the Lord and the gift of eternal life that lies ahead. God's

wisdom is sufficient to guide our thoughts and behaviors that could benefit others.

As we become wise and strong in what we know about God and His Word, we can stand firm on what the Word tells us and can lead others to the great and awesome wonders of God and what His goals are for our lives. We must remember that God made us from His own likeness, therefore, we should align ourselves to conform to what it is He has created us for. He created us to bring Him joy, not ourselves, not your neighbor, not your husband, not your wife, not your mother, not your father, not your child, nobody, but God. Once we have been obedient to God and His Word, then we can receive joy for ourselves. God tells us our joy comes in the morning (Psalm 30:5), and once we have pleased God, He will give us the desires of our hearts.

Protect your mind and heart from the things that are not of God, above all else concentrate on the things that keep you on the straight and narrow path to eternal life. Keep focusing on God and rebuke any distraction or sinful ways that may come against you. Be influenced by nothing but His Word!

Peace and Blessings

Proverbs 5

Um-um. The topic no wants to discuss. Sex. Proverbs 5 tells us that God designed the special covenant of marriage and sex as a gift to married couples for their mutual enjoyment (I Corinthians 7:2-5). Sex outside of marriage can distract one's pursuit to attain wisdom, it destroys family life, erodes a person's ability to love, can be degrading, can lead to disease, result in unwanted pregnancies, and most of all it is against God's law. We must be careful of the cunning words of the promiscuous and resist or refused premarital or unmarried sex. Allow God to move in your life; if He sees fit that you will be in a marital covenant, then it will be. Do not choose or engage with a partner out of your own strength but allow God to choose a partner for you. A man that finds a wife, finds a good thing (Proverbs 18:22), so for us women, your charge is to be all you can be under the direction of God's Word. As for men, when lined up properly with the Word, he will find his treasure and the covenant will be blessed and filled with the happiness and enjoyment that God sees fit for the union.

"Drink from your own well," describes the faithfulness of a marriage. How fitting! In the Old Testament it was a crime to steal water from someone's well, just as it is unjust to have sex with another's wife or husband. The wife or husband should be partaking of their own "well" not of another's. Overall, the excitement and pleasures of sex should be shared by a husband and wife and not encouraged by the enticements or temptations that influence premarital or unmarried sex.

Study HIS WORD, understand the charge on your life, make changes accordingly, and watch how God grants HIS BLESSINGS as opposed to experiencing life in your own strength.

Peace and Blessings

Proverbs 6

Proverbs 6 is direct and in plain English. We are given knowledge of how to be good stewards over money, not to be lazy, things that God detest, and adultery. Verses 1-5 warns of overextending one's self when helping others. Nothing is wrong with helping others, however, we must make wise decisions when committing ourselves to help others as to not deflate oneself. We cannot give or be helpful if we do not have it to give or are unable to be of good help. We must learn a proper balance for our good deeds and day-to-day living.

Laziness brings about struggle. If you are not exerting energy toward life goals and expectations, you will more than likely to not have met all your needs or lack in responsibilities. Work diligently and reap the benefits; be lazy and reap a decline in benefits.

God has set out His Word and Law for all. We must become familiar with God and His Word in order to carry out the charge we have been given. God hates the wicked or sin (Psalm 7:11), and some of the sinful actions or characteristics are haughty eyes, lying, murder, evil, wrongdoing, a false witness, and causing family drama. We must recognize within ourselves as to whether we carry any of these characteristics. If we do, we must begin to resist the temptation and strive to be more like God. We must fill our hearts with the love of God and act accordingly.

When we choose to do God's Will, sin will not be as tempting. However, we must remember that Satan is creatively cunning, therefore, we must seek God daily to direct our path that we may continue to be solid soldiers in His army.

Again, God's Word discusses the covenant between a man and woman. He does not look lightly upon adultery. Adultery can lead to many hurts, fallouts, complications, and a decline in trust. Not only will the adultery affect those intimately involved, but God is also angered. God knows exactly what you need in life. If you run ahead of Him trying or making things happen in your own strength without obeying the Word or consulting Him, you have trashed God's Word and will reap what you sow. Again, drink water from your own well.

Peace and Blessings

Proverbs 7

Proverbs 7 gives clear instructions to stay clear of the promiscuous ways of females (and men are included too). Take heed to the tactics that are used to tempt you – alluring, bold, inviting, cunning, persuasive, attracting, and trapping. These tactics are physically and verbally communicated. RUN! Avoid these tactics and temptations because they ultimately lead to sin.

Women, carry yourselves with respect, dress appropriately, speak with dignity, pray for control over your desires, understand God's Word that you may follow the truth and not be swayed by these things of the world. We are exposed to many things that are not of God and for the most part, we have indulged in them, but we serve a good God. He allows brand new mercies and forgiveness every day. Guard yourself from these things that are tempting. Fill your heart and mind with those things that are of good nature, that are of God. Everything we listen to, read, see, ponder on, or talk about stimulates our actions. Free yourself of sexual desire. In other words, get your mind out the gutter! Treat your body as a prized temple, know that your worth as far more than silver and gold. God dwells within us. Treat His temple with respect and honor.

Self-evaluate. Do you exhibit promiscuous ways? Are you partaking in premarital or unmarried sex? If yes, you're sinning. Let's get right church. There are no excuses.

Let's get right, then go home. Would you want God to call you home before you got right?

Peace and Blessings

Proverbs 8

You got the call, now what are you going to do with it? Proverbs

8 strictly deals with Wisdom. We have discussed multiple times that wisdom comes from God. God has supplied all that we will ever need and His Wisdom can be applied to every aspect of our lives. We must trust and believe that God's Word will direct and guide us daily.

We cannot love God and sin, they do not coexist, it's like water and oil. You must choose God or sin. Even if you choose to continue to sin while pursuing God, you are showing God that you tolerate sin. Remember, He sees and knows all. You may feel you are hiding or keeping a secret pertaining to your sinful ways, but lo and behold, you can't hide from God. Self-evaluate, repent, establish a TRUE relationship with God, and commit yourself to Him completely. The wisdom of God is merely reading, studying, knowing, and applying God's Word. All four steps are imperative to one's relationship with God. He wants you to know Him and interact with Him. God is almighty and only He can do all things, and all things can be possible for us when we put Him first. Do not treat God like He is a second-hand store. We want

to wait until times are hard or troubling before we come to Him. Some like to shop at expensive stores until their money is funny, then they want to hit the smaller retail or second-hand stores that offer mediocre merchandise.

When we have God in our hearts or we go to God and faith, He will supply all our needs, and we know this because we have relied on His Wisdom – His Word – and His Ways. There is only one way to the Father, and that is by Jesus (John 14:6); that's right, Jesus. What has Jesus done for you? What can Jesus do for you? Is your wisdom like His?

Come to know the extreme importance of calling on God and what He has to offer. There is no greater love. Once you experience the greatness of God – attaining wisdom becomes essential and you will yearn for all that God has to offer. It is clear in this chapter that the charge from God is to attain wisdom, and true wisdom comes from HIM. The foundation of our lives is built on this wisdom.

Therefore, take a look at your life, evaluate every aspect, if there is something, anything not right or not aligned with God, seek Him to find the answer. Work to attain wisdom and watch God move in your favor.

We always want what we want in a microwave minute, but we must learn to trust and rest in His timing – we must learn to move with God and not get discouraged. We serve an awesome God.

Peace and Blessings

Proverbs 9

Proverbs 9 portrays wisdom and sin (folly) as women. Both are calling out to you to feed on. Which do you choose? Wisdom, that appeals to the mind, or sin? It is much easier to appeal to senses than it is to rationalize the mind. We must learn to resist what the flesh desires and wants. We must strive to attain more of God's Wisdom, no temptation or trial should deter us from seeking more and more of God's Wisdom. We must also have a personal relationship with God, it's not enough just to know His Word.

Adam and Eve - yup, them two. Look at what happened when they chose to eat from the tree of knowledge of good and evil. Look at the lasting effects that has come about from them eating the forbidden fruit: labor pains, disobedience, a broken relationship with God, and embarrassment. We could go on and on how this choice caused chaos. Self-evaluate, what sin have you partaken in and the effects are still lingering? This is exactly why we must have a relationship God and read His Word DAILY, so that we have godly knowledge and know how to conduct ourselves the way God wants us to. We must remember that our time here on Earth is a spiritual battle, you cannot fight a spiritual battle with the flesh or a spirit that lacks knowledge.

We must take heed to God's Word, APPLY and PUT INTO ACTION what we know and have learned about God in His Word. I heard you – how do you put a spiritual battle into action? With the Word. When something comes up against you, you must be able to recall God's Word and apply it to handle day-to-day living or any situation.

Every answer you need is found right there in your BIBLE and in prayer. What if you don't know where to look? That is exactly why you must study to show YOURSELF approved. Read God's Word like you talk on the phone, reply on social media, watch TV, or read other books. No one can put God's Word in your heart like your own eyes and mind. Seek out a spiritual counselor that is trustworthy and knows the Word of God to give guidance. In addition, PRAY!

Pray for wisdom, pray in faith, believe that what you are asking God for shall come to pass. God is a faithful God – are you reciprocating that faithfulness? If not, try HIM, He loves you and He would love to have regular communication with you. He made you in His own likeness, He knows everything about you, even the number of hairs on your head. He is the ultimate protector, guidance counselor, healer, giver, and He is also in the blessing business.

Who else can give you all of that and then some!? Overall, God is merciful and loves us, so now is the time. Start a love affair with God...there is nothing like it. There is no greater love – not your father, mother, child, brother, sister, man, woman, relative, friend, or

associate. There is nobody that can do you like God!

I am so humbled that God uses me. He has done an awesome work in my life, and I stand to share all that He has done for me. By no means have my accomplishments or calling on my life come from me, but from the God that is in me. I trust Him, I love Him, and I give Him all of the Praise. God is so good, I will, I do, I am available for Him. I thank God and all that I say and do. There is nobody like my God! Thank You, God. Thank YOU! Hallelujah to His name!

Peace and Blessings

Proverbs 10

Two days in a row Wisdom has called out to give you insight of choice. Well today, Proverbs 10 provides tidbits for applying Wisdom to everyday living. We know right from wrong, but are we living it? The Word is repetitive in the manner that we can grasp what we are reading and given examples to get clarity. Long to be Christ-like, don't be lazy, avoid negative situations or aspects that influence sinful ways, bridle the tongue, and strive to live righteous.

Communicate with God, allow your heart to be unhardened that you are open to His Word with careful consideration not to be bamboozled by wolves in sheep's clothing. Understand that your thoughts or opinions will not ever reach that of God's but know that we can attain an abundance of knowledge and wisdom that draws us closer to God. God is almighty and all powerful. Our little pea brains could not fathom God's stature. However, through His Word we can grow to be more like HIM.

What better way to grow but through His Word. It's all right there in a nice little bound package that has remained the same yesterday, today, and forever. Read, study, and apply. I'll say it again, read, study, and apply. Seize the opportunity to live diligently for Him and you will reap what He has for you. Let the Son shine in, face it with a grin, open up your heart, and let the Son shine in!

Peace and Blessings

Proverbs 11

Aww, the scales of life. Does the good nature in you outweigh the bad? Proverbs 11 discusses the contrast between good or living right and the bad, evil or living wrong. How we conduct ourselves in behavior and with our words, bring about life or death with oneself and others. Our conduct with both also decides our fate.

Are we headed for destruction or construction? When we exhibit wrongdoings unto others, gossip, rely on riches, or detest God's Word, we are headed for self-destruction. When we exhibit helpfulness, control of the tongue, rely on God and make daily efforts to live according to the Word, we are in construction. A change is being made from what we were or currently in concerning our spiritual walks, and advancing to another level of Christ-likeness. We must begin to walk upright and stop complaining or waddling in what we are going through. We must learn to PICK UP OUR BIBLES and exercise our minds, tongues, and actions to reflect the Word.

I Peter 3:15 tells us we must always be ready to proclaim God's

Word. Are you ready? If not, get ready. Come to know God and His Word on a more personal level to show thyself approved. Our goal is to be more Christ-like and stop using the excuses of "I don't understand the Bible. I don't have enough time in the day. I'm tired. I'm sleepy. I had a long day or night." My response to that – WHATEVER! What if God gave you all those excuses when you call on Him? Rely on the God in you to be the conductor of your path. Make the necessary changes in your life to get on track and serve God as He has instructed and as your heart should desire. Read the words of the chapter carefully, think about how you interact and speak. Are you fueling the light of God within yourself that you may continue to shine, or are you becoming snuffed out with deception and the temptations of the world? Pray that God does a mighty work within you, that you may exhibit the Christ-likeness that He delights in.

The word for the day: ACTION! Get the Word in you and put it into ACTION!

Peace and Blessings

Proverbs 12

How can we know God's Word? We can come to know God's Word through our reading and studying of the Word. Many may read the Word, but do they study? To learn, we must study to get a thorough comprehension of what we are reading. We must structure and become stable in our studying with discipline and be accepting of correction and constructive criticism. We must remember the path that Jesus traveled to the cross was a hard road to travel, but He pressed on because His death had to happen for our salvation.

Now we must do the same in our studying. We must be diligent in our reading and studying. Our study journey may get daunting at times, but we must stay the course. We must keep pressing on like Jesus did on the road to the cross. Like His death gave us our salvation, we should be obedient in our studying and bring joy to God.

We can be encouraged because our awesome God has given us His Word and the tools to attain the knowledge and instructions we need to survive.

Peace and Blessings

Proverbs 13

My oh my!!!! There are a bunch of goodies in today's reading. There are six points that I would like to touch on. The first is from Verse 6: the paths of obedience or disobedience - Which one will you take?

The path of obedience to God develops order in our lives. With His Word we are safeguarded against anything that could come against us. If the path of disobedience is chosen, it will lead to confusion and destruction (Didn't we just talk about this? Repetitiveness makes for accessible recall).

Verse 10 - EEEWWWWW-WEEEEE. Can you say pride? Humility? Pride reflects one's own dignity and if not checked, it can become boastful and stir up conflict and division. We must realize that we ARE NOT PERFECT, when we make bad decisions or rely on pride, we tend not to own up to our OWN faults or mistakes. Instead of relying on pride, humble thyself! Allow yourself the wisdom or advice of a trusted person to help correct wrongdoing or recognize your pride is in the way. Acknowledging prideful ways will allow us to humble ourselves and alleviate stress, the urge to lash out, or to stop having those pity parties.

Verse 17 speaks of giving and receiving messages and communication. When we communicate, it must be done in love, honesty, and not to mislead. We must choose what we say, as to be respectful and to avoid misunderstanding. In the event that consideration is not taken when communicating, your very words, conversation, or message may be damaging to relationships or cause quarrels. If you don't have anything good to say or if you know what you are communicating is not the truth, shut up! Be swift to hear and slow to speak!

Verse 19 tells us it is possible to dream or achieve goals, especially if it is worthwhile. If we use wrongdoing or evil ways to achieve those dreams or goals, will those dreams or goals be tainted? Is it worthwhile? I think not, God does not do confusion and tossing in aspects that are not of God, will not prosper. Desire your dreams and goals with and through our Father and watch how He makes things come to pass, in His time, not on our, "I can make it happen" time.

EXTRA EXTRA - You read all about it!!!! Once again, we are told to be cautious of who we call friend. We must surround ourselves with like-minded, with those who are on the same path, and those who cherish the personal and intimate relationship with Christ. When we surround ourselves with these types of friends, we can learn from each other, lean on each other without feeling burdensome, speak from the depths of our belly and grow in faith with each other.

Iron sharpens iron (Proverbs 27:17). In other words, the meeting of the minds, providing new insight, refinement, and stimulating each other's mind to become sharper. And my last point. Verse 24, beat'em! (lol, just kidding). But for real, we must discipline our children! Our job as parents is to nurture and provide guidance for our children. We can do this through the teaching of God's Word, the teaching of life lessons, and disciplining them when they have discarded what they have learned. The lack of discipline leaves leeway for the child or children to think they have gotten away with his or her wrongdoing. Without discipline or correction, the child or children may not have a clear understanding of right from wrong. We cannot beat wisdom into our children but encourage it through TEACHING them. This means you actually need to spend time and talk with them regularly. We must encourage our children to know God for themselves. However, when the child needs a spanking for his or her wrongdoing, it must be done in love and correction.

Peace and Blessings

Proverbs 14

Is it sticking yet? What? The importance of attaining wisdom from God. Proverbs dishes out vast scenarios of wisdom versus sinful ways or manners. Read them carefully, adhere to the words being read and put them into thought and action.

Three points stood out to me. Serving God, seeking wisdom, and controlling the temper.

Verse 4 describes that a stable (your life) can be clean without o x (others) in it to wreak havoc (dirty it up). However, without others, who would we interact with to be built up spiritually, or carry out the charge given by God? We are not to live empty lives, but to encourage one another in faith, service, and justice.

Your life can be a witness to others by them seeing you operate in faith – studying and applying God's Word on a daily basis. Your service will be evident in the manner you carry out the call on your life and how you treat others in their time of need. Justice will be revealed when you stay honest and mindful to right and wrong and carry out the proper responses to situations. Collectively, these points exhibit service to God.

Verse 6 describes many believers who are still struggling with what he or she finds to be the truth. Those that stumble over every wind of doctrine, advise, or instruction only stumble because they have not sought out wisdom for themselves. Some know just enough to state that they believe, but always have a "What if" or "that ain't what I was told" or "I believe...(and have no recourse of proof)." Attaining wisdom is not magical, nor can other believers give it to you. You must attain God's Wisdom for yourself. Again, attaining wisdom involves READING and STUDYING God's Word.

In addition, establish a true relationship with God through prayer. If it seems hard to attain wisdom, even when given the steps to do so, maybe a self-evaluation is in order. Could it be your attitude? One's attitude can be a deterrent from attaining the truth and wisdom because of the mental block he or she may have, the unwillingness to do your part in the relationship, impatience, or the stubbornness that claims all of your time that could really have been spent with God. What is truly holding you back from gaining the wisdom of God? He offers it, what are you going to do to get it?

And verse 29 - EEEWWWWW-WEEEEE! The temper! The temper can be defined as the tendency to become easily angered. A nasty temper can relinquish bitterness and hastiness, two attributes that exhibit negativity. Bitterness reveals one's anger or dislike and will show in one's attitude, judgment, actions, and will definitely show on his or her face. Hastiness shows impatience or hurriedness, which ultimately reveals that one's action is done in a manner that was not thoroughly considered. In this event, bad or wrong decisions could be made, or the response could be insulting. AGAIN – self-evaluate!

What is the cause of such a short, quick, nasty temper? Anger can be a legit response to injustice or sin; however, temper should be controlled to allow for reasoning of what has caused the anger. Is your temper due to some selfish

belief or "the way you are" or "not what you believe" or "not what you would have done." Well, guess what? You are one of many, and all that you say, do, or believe does not mean others do too. We must become more respectful of others and allow for their opinions or beliefs to be heard. We may not agree, but just as God has given us choice, another has a choice of what they say, do, or believe. If you cannot handle what others say, do, or believe, AGAIN, check yourself. We live in a world of differences. We can agree to disagree, in fact, if you give leeway to that short temper, you might just learn something!

We can take what we need from conversations or situations and leave what we don't. No need to get upset. Becoming upset and living in this manner seems to defeat who God has called you to be. God is of good-nature, joy, and prosperity. How can one experience these attributes if your temper is short fused? What if everyone you deal with has a short fused temper? How would you feel? The next time you find your temper kicking in, think of how you are affecting those you are snapping on and how God would judge your actions. Were your actions Christ-like? Check your temper, seek wisdom, that you may serve God in the way He intended!

Peace and Blessings

Proverbs 15

Whew!!! Proverbs 15 can be a month long Bible study! I mean to tell ya. I will only speak of 5 points, although I could probably go verse for verse. First off is verse one, "kill'em with kindness," is one of my favorite sayings. In other words, we can kill one's evil, mad, angry, hasty motives, speech, or actions with loving kindness.

Instead of letting our temper represent who we are, we can use kind words that SHOULD be set in our hearts. Using our soft, indoor voice can be very irritating and confusing to those who are angry, negative, or pessimistic. Allowing others to see that we trust in God's Word and rely on Him to diffuse situations or conversations will cause one to check his or

herself or at least recognize that he or she is the only one getting bent out of shape. Console the situation or conversation with those kind words and keep it moving and watch how the situation dissolves or the conversation turns around. When we know and exhibit the love of God, anger takes a backseat to what we can accomplish with His Word and the words that come out of our mouths. Ponder it people, live an abundant, not a defeated life.

Verses 5 and 32 are telling us that we must learn from correction. For the most part, people know when they have done wrong or have sinned, do not allow this wrongdoing or sin to go uncorrected. Beat down your pride and humble yourself.

Allow correction in your life. Grow. As a planted seed needs water for nourishment to grow, correction is like a fertilizer that promotes one's withering growth. Do not be offended but accepting. You might learn something!

In addition, correction must be done in love. There is nothing mean or nasty about assisting or helping another see the error of his or her ways. Recognizing the wrong or sin is the first step, confessing with one's mouth is next, and then actually rectifying the error or inaccuracy will assist in building one's character and wisdom. Correction is not to beat you up or to boast of one's knowledge, but to encourage and create a notion of honesty with one's self. If errors, mistakes, or inaccuracies go without corrections, this may contribute to failing or living defeated.

Verse 12 backs this up. People do not care to be corrected. Without correction, you will have no moral constraints on your behavior or thoughts, let alone how you tame the tongue. As you can see, there are no inconsistencies in God's Word. He has given us His Word to abide by, telling us right from wrong, good from bad, nice from naughty, up from down, all that, we must take heed to correction. We must learn to recognize our flaws and allow correction to be the motivation to get back on track and leave behind stubbornness, complacency, and bad attitude.

Verse 14 tells us we are what we eat. If we feed our spirit and

mind those things that are not of God, that is exactly how we will carry ourselves. I DO NOT CARE IF YOU CLAIM YOU GOT IT UNDER CONTROL! You cannot serve God and sin. What we read, listen to, talk about, or watch are part of our mental diet. When the mind is giving garbage (sinful thoughts, bad thoughts, etc.), it becomes influenced by those very things. We must take careful consideration of what we feed our minds, then we can become spiritually healthy in our thoughts. We can nurture ourselves with the goodness of God's Word and reap well-being in our words and actions.

Lastly, Verse 15. The attitude! Attitude can be defined as a settled way of thinking or feeling about someone or something, typically one that is reflected in a person's behavior. So, if you wake up every day feeling there is always something negative going to happen or every day brings trouble, you will carry yourself in that manner (negative). If you use your wisdom in expecting that you will encounter tests or trials AND knowing that God has made leeway for us to conquer any tests or trials, we can live happily. There is nothing that can come up against us that God has not given us an outlet. Our minds must be stayed on the goodness of God and all that He has to offer us. In knowing this, we can choose our attitude. We cannot control what happens on the day-to-day basis, but we can choose the attitude in how we deal with any encounter, situation, or conversation. When your heart has been filled with the love of God, He becomes the foundation of our thoughts, words, and actions, thus leading to a Christ-like attitude. How do you choose to operate, with an attitude of defeat or an attitude of Christ-likeness?

Peace and Blessings

Proverbs 16

Proverbs 16 is a reminder of our ability to choose insight of our part in the covenant with God while on our life's journey. Versus 1, 3, and 9 speak of the freedom to plan or make plans. A plan is a detailed proposal of doing or achieving something, and if we want a plan

to come to pass in a prosperous or completed manner, we must include God. God will decline or grant the proposal we set before HIM. Even if we don't include God, He still has the last say, He determines our steps. Therefore, it is essential that we consult with God in everything that we do. God knows what is best for us and He will allow us to devise efforts towards our dreams, desires, or whatever it is we are aspiring, but we must have God in it. We must put our faith and trust in Him knowing that He makes all things possible, and our plans will come to light when we have shown obedience and faithfulness – which is God's delight.

Be of good-nature and press toward life satisfaction through Jesus and exercise the Word God has given us to survive in this world. We must draw on what we know to be right and true, to share the Good News, and stand up against the fiery darts and snares that come against us. We must use godly discretion in making any move, decision, plan, or conversation. We must be in tune with God and allow Him to guide us in our discretions. We must allow Him to be the head of our actions and decisions. The wisdom that we receive from God and His Word can and will conquer all. We must not be afraid to go to God. He tells us in His scripture: Let us therefore come boldly unto the throne of grace, that we may obtain mercy, and find grace to help in time of need (Hebrews 4:16). We must recognize that we need God every minute of every day and when we are making decisions, we must remember to consult with God to learn what is best for us. In other words, seek God in everything about yourself and what you say and do.

Peace and Blessings

Proverbs 17

Proverbs 17 is an overview of previous chapters and insight for godly instruction. Going through tests and trials, learning to speak when appropriate, with the appropriate words and timing; helping those in need, being a good friend, and seeking God in all that we do are characteristics that we must polish within

ourselves. Scriptures go over and over the Good News and life instructions that are critical for our relationship with God and to be Christ-like in nature. Tests and trials are like fire testing the purity of silver or gold – I Peter 1:7 tells us that our faith is far more than mere gold. However, pressing through these tests and trials exhibit one's faith.

Relying on God in true faith will give you leverage to accomplish or surpass any tests or trials. As your faith matures and the lessons learned from what you went through must not be forgotten. This maturing faith will help you continually press forward and allow for testimonies for others. Bridling the tongue is also a vital aspect for growing in Christ, as well as witnessing or interacting with others. Understanding that there is life and death in the tongue, we must be careful what we say, how we say it, and when to state what it is we want to express.

Encouragement with God's Word may save someone's life; discouragement with a wild tongue may bring havoc or drama to a person or situation. We must learn to take a backseat to our own overwhelming opinions and attitudes and practice wisdom, honesty, patience, and love in a manner that is conducive to Christ-likeness, and that speaks life.

Helping those in need can involve many aspects. As a believer, we can help someone with the words we speak, monetary donations, assistance with one's household or home life, sharing the Gospel, or giving someone a ride. The point is that our heart should be of good character so that we may be able to discern the appropriate assistance or help that another may need. We must become sensitive to the people of God that are in need and help build them up spiritually that they may learn to trust in God that their needs can be met.

Loyalty to one another is a big task, as believers, must learn that everyone is not our "friend" but those who are a "friend" to us must have characteristics that reflect Christ-like motives, actions, and words. A friend is as close as a brother. A friend would not lead you astray but encourage you with God's Word. A friend can be honest with you without being offensive. A friend is one who has put God first in their own lives, as well as how they operate or communicate in this world. When we encounter a person of this nature, we can call them friend, time out for drama or games. God's work must be done. We must begin to put in action the very things that we learned from God's Word and treat each other with dignity and respect, keeping in mind to whom we call friend.

When we seek God, and all that we do, we are gaining insight from the BEST! God is omniscient and no other answer or way is better than His!

Peace and Blessings

Proverbs 18

This chapter gives us insight on the fool, the fool's tongue, and the fool's actions. We must remember that we are still "children" of Christ, and we must check our speech and behaviors accordingly. Are the actions and words we use on a regular basis giving glory unto God? Even in irregular instances, do we practice Christ-likeness?

We must become numb to the things that are not of God and that do not represent Him. We must show ourselves to be in the army of the Lord, clothed with His Word and characteristics, that the God in us is seen through our words and behaviors.

When we trust God, obey God, and give praise unto God, He will direct our paths, He will give us the strength to muster forward, He can make all things possible. See where I'm going with this? Right! You could be a fool without God. Our every move, word, breath, or blink is because of God. He has also given us free will; we have the opportunity to line up with His word and His nature to see past the things that could influence foolish living. Bring God glory through the manner in which you live, show thyself approved through His Word, and rely on Him for EVERYTHING!

Don't say another word or make another move without consulting God first. Yes, He already knows, but He wants you to communicate with Him. Keep your mind stayed on Him and your Christ-like actions will follow. There is no greater love or source of wisdom.

Peace and Blessings

Proverbs 19

OK, so how many more times will you have to be told before you get it? God tells us things again and again, why? SO THAT YOU WILL GET IT! We read the words of scripture and feel the jolt for that moment, then continue on in our own or fleshly ways. God knows this, He knows all, so why do you think you are tricking Him?

Remember the Trix commercial? Trix are for kids. Well that's exactly what God is saying when we do not take heed and adhere to what His Word instructs. We have our nice little world (the bowl of cereal) and satisfied with the colorful content (the different colors of the cereal represent the different things going on in our lives) resting in milk (God). We smashed through the bowl of cereal in record time without hesitation (living life carelessly without consideration); with every bite, there was a little bit of God in it, and once the cereal was gone, there was some saving grace left, the milk we drink at the end. Did you get full? Which was more filling, the cereal or the milk at the end? Think about it before you answer. Right, you were more fulfilled in the end because the milk was the last sweet savor before you could say "I'm done." So go ahead kids, eat your Trix, but use a bigger spoon so that more of God is in it and eventually you will exchange that cereal for a sandwich (sandwich - God the bread, His Word the meat, and the Holy Spirit is the mayo).

Think about it again. Can you get full on that? What I am trying to say saints is that we must not only read His Word, but we must also put into action the lessons learned, and we must eat of His Word to fill us with that of the Father.

Peace and Blessings

Proverbs 20

Proverbs 20 is an "ouch" chapter, putting the mirror in your face. Look at yourself. Are you living honest and according to God's Word? Many valuable lessons are

in Chapter 20: not to be drunk, avoid fights and quarrels, don't be lazy, be reliable, don't have double standards, be trusting, be trustworthy, do not steal, do not gossip, seek wise advice, the Lord directs our paths, be honest, and discipline purifies the heart. Now how many (this isn't even all that the chapter talks about) characteristics are alive in you today? How do you encompass these characteristics?

As believers and followers of Christ, we must recognize that all we are (the good and the bad) in Christ; and clean up and align our lives according to the Word. We are quick to recognize the good in ourselves or make ourselves look good, but what happens to those things in us that are not perfect? That are not of God? That are not Christ-like? That are just dead wrong? Things must be brought to our remembrance to keep us intact and humble. This is exactly why we should have a personal, daily relationship with our Maker! God directs our paths and gives us strength to carry on; He gives us brand new mercies and forgiveness. We will only live defeated in this world if we choose to, for God is our fortress (Psalm 18:1-3) - our strong, secure refuge.

We can look to the hills which cometh our help (Psalm 121:1)... we must begin to move when God moves, obey His Word, get fire under our feet and put ACTION TO SCRIPTURE. You can talk a good game, but can you walk it?

Peace and Blessings

Proverbs 21

Proverbs 21 should be read carefully. As with most of Proverbs, there are comparisons of the lifestyles of the righteous and the wicked. The comparisons are usually those that are an outlook on life, responses to life situations, how one is seen by others, and the quality of life that one leads. The righteous are usually hopeful, concerned, blessed, respected, respectful, cares, against dishonesty and evil, happy for others in their accomplishments, stand firm in God's Word and strays from those who are not like-minded. On the other hand, the wicked are cruel, not thoroughly understanding, linked with violence and evil ways, headed for destruction, dishonest, trapped by evil ambitions, and not concerned. Think about these characteristics in comparison to who YOU are. Which characteristics best describe you?

Again, this is why it is so imperative to know God's Word for yourself. Striving to be Christ-like takes will and determination to press through wickedness or wicked ways. We must strive to present ourselves holy and acceptable to Christ, which is our REASONABLE service (Romans 12:1). We must begin to stand strong and bold for WHO we honor and worship and that is GOD alone! We learn from our mistakes, we gain knowledge from like-minded people, we attain wisdom from God, we must exhibit true loving motives of the heart, we must say and live what we believe. Our focus must be stayed on God, rely on HIM in all thy ways, become FAITHFUL TO GOD, get the Word engrafted into our hearts, that our light should shine of HIS glory. When His Word is in us, our actions and words become of Him. Now the questions. When people see you, do they see Christ?

Are the scales unbalanced? Which weighs more, righteousness or wickedness?

I am praying for all: *Father God we thank You once again that we are able to wake another day that we may serve You. I pray that we are able to indulge in Your Word so that it becomes the daily instruction of our lives, that we may do the greater work that You have called us to do, and that we may be righteous in Your eyes. We stand firm knowing that You are our Creator and that You know all, so we ask that You condition our hearts to veer from wickedness and the trials of this world, that we may be strong contenders in this spiritual battle. I pray for strength and understanding for all who are coming unto You, give them a mind and heart to want more of You. You are amazing, You are awesome, and You are almighty. We thank You Lord, we give You all the praise and honor, we lift Your name on high. Bless us as only You can and we ask all this in Your precious Son's name, Amen!*

Peace and Blessings

Proverbs 22

Proverbs 22 is like part 2 of Proverbs 21, the Word is telling us to shape up and follow God. We are given multiple examples of how not to be and what we should do to avoid stumbling. One of the verses that stood out for me today was verse 6. This verse tells us to direct or train our children onto the right path and as they get older, they will not leave it. Today's parents do not sit and talk with their children, they talk to them in passing or very briefly. Some of our grandmas were the epitome of this very tactic that is needed. Grandma would SIT you down and explain the no-no and give a thorough explanation why, usually taking up all the play time. Well parents, it's our turn.

We must begin to speak life into your children, get them in tune with God's Word and Ways. Stop using excuses for why we don't bring our children to church. Teach them life lessons or talk and teach them about the ways of the world. We are responsible, WE ARE RESPONSIBLE (oops, did I say that twice?). Not only must we keep a tab on our own responsibility with our spirituality and with life, but with our children as well. What excuses have you poured out to explain why you haven't or why you don't? Stop running from the truth and start now before it's too late. If you love your children, do for them what God has done for you.

Peace and Blessings

Proverbs 23

Well look here! The "NOT" chapter. Chapter 23 has a repetitiveness with using the word "not." To negate from or the absence of, defines "not."

We are given insight into what to do and what not to do. We must have a daily conscious of right from wrong, do's and don'ts, and stand firm against temptation. We listen to or see things in our lives over and over; some learn lessons from life experiences and others do not. In the event that nothing is learned, we continue on in the same manner that could possibly be the exact hindrance to gaining or productivity. We must begin to be honest with ourselves and recognize that

flaws and the"nots" in life that keep us from what God has for us.

Remember that God gets His glory out of our obedience; Are you giving God glory? Draw closer to God, long for His comfort and soft words. He is your Daddy, Father, Abba, Maker, and Creator. He said He would never leave you nor forsake you, therefore, you can stand against the "nots" of this world. No matter how hard, how bad, how long, how discouraging... God Can! God is able like no other, trust in HIM, lean on HIM, get to know HIM and He will NOT fail you!

Peace and Blessings

Proverbs 24

Proverbs 24 round up Chapters 10-23. These chapters basically give insight of wisdom for all people. Chapter 24 tells us that wisdom must be attained to build our lives prosperously. Wisdom becomes the very tool we use to strengthen our thoughts, motives, prayers, and behaviors. We must rely on what the Word says, stand firm on it and begin to use wisdom in all of our conversations, actions, interactions, and decisions. Wise decisions must be thought out, allowing room for evaluation and alternatives before deciding. God only wants what is best for us, therefore, we must consult with Him with every move we make, every breath we take, that God may direct our paths. If we should choose the wrong path or stumble, we must regroup and allow God and His Word to work within us that we may reciprocate His goodness. We are not perfect, but we can go to God who is! Stop using excuses, CHANGE your ways that are not conducive to godly living, use your tests and trials for maturing and learning, PRACTICE what you read in the Word, worry no more, but trust in the Lord with all your heart. For what shall it profit a man, if he shall gain the whole world, and lose his own soul? (Mark 8:36). Stop deceiving others and yourself. Turn to God in all things, for all things are possible with Him as well as protection and security. He said He would never leave us nor forsake us. God is calling you. Are you going to answer? When you knock on His door, will He answer?

Peace and Blessings

Proverbs 25

Proverbs 25 is talking to you, that is if you are a leader or a soldier for Christ. We must begin to look like and act like who God has called us to be. We must become in tune with the call on our lives and act accordingly. God makes no mistakes, therefore, if there is a mistake or something is not right, who's to blame? Yes, I heard you, you are not to blame for all things that happen to you, however, when situations do occur that come up against God's Will for your life or lives around you, you can rest in knowing that God has not given us the spirit of fear, but of power and of love and of a sound mind (II Timothy 1:7). That's right, sound mind!!!!! We must use the godly discretion in all things, not one or some, but ALL! We become leaders or soldiers for Christ through our actions and words, our light will shine when God has been put first. The quality of one's life draws attention. Attention to what? To one's trustworthiness, patience, kindness, dedication, and honesty.

We cannot lead others to Christ when we are not modeling the goodness of Christ and all that He is. He is marvelous, all powerful, almighty, sovereign, and supreme.

Every ounce of steam we have in us, should be used to glorify our God. We learn, attain, and gain our Christ-likeness from communion with Him, prayer, fellowship with like-minded, and living according to His Word. Self-evaluate. Are you missing any attribute that could slow your roll with Jesus? Are you the leader God has called you to be? It's time, get right and don't let the encounters of this world, tests, or trials snuff out your light!

Peace and Blessings

Proverbs 26

Control. The word for the day is control. Proverbs 26 give multiple examples of the control we need to have over our tongue and behaviors. Instead of lashing out or speaking before we think, we must have consideration in all individual situations, that we can make good judgment of how to respond.

The right words and timing are imperative to getting across what it is you are trying to say or do. We must have knowledge and wisdom as our guide in speaking and in conducting ourselves. KNOW that life has tests, trials, and things that come up against us or others. Stop acting as though they don't or won't. Instead, be prepared. You must be built up with God's Word and Wisdom to overcome these very tests, trials, or whatever has come against us or others. We must have our attitudes become like Jesus. Did He lash out? Did He turn His back on you? Did He give up because He was overwhelmed, or it got to be too much for Him? This is where the bigger questions are posed. What Would Jesus Do? Do you know what He would do? Well, if you don't, you should. Control is defined as the ability or power to manage or restrain. What godly control are you exhibiting daily?

Peace and Blessings

Proverbs 27

Proverbs 27 is a clear, cut-throat passage that influences

self-evaluation. The topics that stood out to me were praise, friends, debate, and thoughts. In this chapter, praise refers to compliments that one may receive. Praise is given for approval or admiration. However, praise is not to be confused with boasting or to glorify one's self. Praise for another is merely a compliment to someone's actions, deeds, kind behaviors, or sound advice. When one receives praise, he or she must know that whatever he or she has done to receive it is not of his or her own strength, but what God has allowed as a talent, witness, gift, or of His greater work. We can do all things because of Who God is, not because God actually used YOU for the purpose He did. When you receive praise, be respectful and accepting, and in return YOU give God His praise. All we do is because of God - and what a God we serve!

In the Bible, there are several Scriptures about "friends." These Scriptures tell us to be very considerate of who we choose as a "friend." This friend will be loyal and closer than a brother and when the relationship can withstand that special bond throughout the good and bad times, you have found a friend in your brethren. The loyalty of this friend will exhibit a true-heart, reliability, dependability, and trustworthiness. In regard to these characteristics, friendships can withstand trials, oppositions, and egotistical personalities. Furthermore, the friendship will be accepting of constructive criticism and new ideas or ways. As scripture tells us, iron sharpens iron. Friends can build each other up, refine thoughts, give clarity to situations or give insight. This is also why the Bible tells us to surround ourselves with people who are like-minded and Christ-like.

Debating, arguing, quarreling, not agreeing, whatever you want to call it, is not of God. God does not do confusion. If there is an issue at hand, learn to keep a calm spirit, become an active listener and find a more effective way of communicating what you want or what needs to be said. If you disagree, get proof. If you are unable to provide proof, make an effort to find out for YOURSELF what's really in the pudding.

Furthermore, constant, loud nagging is irritating and usually provides no resolution. PATIENCE WORKETH FAITH. Knowing that God is in your heart is sufficient enough to step away from the chaos and let God and His Word cover the situation. If you have a point to prove, it can be done in love and kindness. When you approach it in a negative aspect, you have already been defeated. Philippians 2:5 tell us to let the mind (thoughts) be in you, which was also in Christ Jesus; and Philippians 4:8 states whatsoever things are true, honest, just, pure, lovely, of good reputation, any virtue, any praise, to think on these things. Therefore, if your thoughts are not of the stated characteristics, those very thoughts may bring strife, damnation, sin, grief, and other negative outcomes.

As we mature in our walk, our Bible reading and studying will assist in renewing our mind or thoughts. Romans 12:2 says be ye transformed by the renewing of your mind. We must change the old way we used to think, we must be strong in faith to not be conformed to the old ways or the ways of the world, but to strive for what is good, acceptable, perfect, and the Will of God (Romans 12:2). We must recognize the difference between the Spirit and the flesh. We must battle the flesh, that it may not rise but allow the Spirit to move within. When this happens, we become light or can live in a manner that is conducive to God's Will. God has given us all that we need to obey and honor Him. It is our responsibility to nourish the Spirit and be on one accord with the Word, which are our instructions for LIFE. Through His Word, we learn to renew our mind, no longer will those negative, pessimistic thoughts override what is engrafted into our Christ-like hearts.

The time is NOW. Accept Christ into your heart, give Him room to work in you, speak death unto those old fleshly ways, come boldly before the throne, as you are one of God's children and the victory is yours. We know the battle here on Earth is won, so until we get to Heaven, we must continue to do the work of God. (*Repost for Psalm 55*).

Peace and Blessings

Proverbs 28

Proverbs 28 continues to give us insight into the change that should be occurring on the inside. The way that we behave and communicate deals with internal matters. The way we think, speak, react, interact, and abide is all controlled through the physiology of our bodies. Our bodies learn and grow from what we feed it and do for it. When we feed our bodies the nourishing Word of God, our thoughts, communication, behaviors, and obedience begin to reflect that. We cannot see impulses of information flowing from nerve to nerve throughout our bodies, but we can identify with the manner in which we feed our internal selves. We can accomplish this with the Word. God's Word provides the love and wisdom that influences our spirit to thirst for Him. The more you are in tune with the Word, the tighter your relationship with God. Read this chapter again and reflect on situations that correlate with what the scripture is telling you.

One last thing, Verse 9 stands out to me. "One who turns away his ear from hearing the law, even his prayer is an abomination." Need it even simpler? God detests prayers of one who ignores the law (His Word). Now that is HEAVY!!! Your communication may be on block if you're carrying on and such, acting like you don't know. Remember, you are responsible for what you know, so don't get frustrated when you feel your prayers are in limbo. Go to our Father right, you can't hide anything from Him anyway.

Do some meditation, soul searching, call on God, get right, START, MAKE AN EFFORT, ACTION, MOVE, DO IT FOR REAL. Make necessary changes in your life, changes that line up with God's Word, you KNOW what they are. (*Repost from Psalm 63-65*)

Peace and Blessings

Proverbs 29

Proverbs 29 speaks a multitude of self-evaluation. Three topics were prevalent for me, disciplining children, divine guidance, and God-fearing. Although Proverbs 29 has a lot to say other than those three topics, these three are lessons to be stored in our repertoire. Disciplining our children is imperative for their maturation, their knowledge of right from wrong and of God's Word. When we discipline our children, we must use measures appropriate for misbehaving. Children sometimes deserve a spanking for his or her actions, but they also need the knowledge of WHY they are being disciplined. Merely punishing them is not enough, we must also communicate with our children, giving them the understanding of how we have chosen to raise them and to have them familiar with what God expects of them. Not everyone raises their children the same way, so we as the parents must make clear what is expected of our children and the relationship that we and our families have with God. When one is told what is expected of them, they are now held accountable for knowing. If they are not aware of what is expected, usually they find out when something bad or negative has happened to bring about a punishment. So we must TALK to our children, not just when they get in trouble, but daily, teaching them life lessons that will keep them from doing wrong or repeating wrongs. The parent/child relationship is a loving covenant. If we love our children like we say we do, then discipline will not be difficult, because through our love for them, we will enlighten them in our and God's expectations. We must also remember that we all fall short, but when the knowledge and wisdom of God is intertwined; the child will remember in which way they should go (Proverbs 22:6).

Verse 18 states that if there is no vision, people will perish. The vision in this verse can be translated as "revelation," which in turn means "divine guidance." If we do not acknowledge God and His Word, we tend to just be or running wild, but when we are in tune with God and His Word, we have a reverence for Him and His Word and will conduct our lives accordingly. Furthermore, vision or divine guidance enhances our perception of what will occur or be produced if a certain course is followed.

Thus, it increases our discernment and sharpens our judgment about which way we should go. Overall, vision gives a mental picture of results and If the vision seems good to a person, that person will be motivated to proceed in their "visualized" direction.

God-fearing is basically stating that you believe in God and His Word with a deep compassion. Anything that goes against God or His Word makes you fearful, you respect and reverence God and His authority, and because you know His Word, you know the consequences of disobedience or neglect of His Word.

Proverbs 1:7, Proverbs 9:10, Proverbs 15:33, Job 28:20, and Ecclesiastes 12:13-14 speaks of the fear of the Lord. Enough said! God's Word tells us that all are called but few are chosen. If all are called, then why are only a few chosen? This is because NOT ALL those who were called are willing to make a choice to walk that narrow path. Are you chosen?

Peace and Blessings

Proverbs 30

What a wonderful day in the Lord! God is so awesome He can bring back what you thought you lost or help you to lose what you don't need. With that being said, there are things in life that we sometimes don't understand. When we don't understand them, we start to lean on our own understanding and as we know, sometimes our own understanding is not the route to go. There are also things in life that may seem unimaginable, those very things that God and only God can make happen or make sense of.

Proverbs 30 gives us insight on the things that seem to be a stretch from our understanding and those things that we can or cannot imagine. Verse 5 can sum it all up for you, that every word of God proves true. THANK YOU JESUS!!!!! Everything we ever need or need to know is housed right there in our Bible, and it's TRUE!!! Look no more, God is in the house! He is so awesome! He can hold the wind in His fist, He created the WHOLE world, and He made every living creature. Isn't that enough to get excited about?! If my God, your God, our God can do those things, just think what He can do with an obedient child! Get in His Word, get excited, He is an awesome God, rain or shine, He Can! God is not a man that He should tell a lie, if HE said it is so, on Him you can rely!

Peace and Blessings

Proverbs 31

Proverbs 31 starts off speaking of drunkenness. Alcohol clouds the mind and leads to bad judgment or actions. Many of us have had our drunken nights and have acted totally out of character. That is not how Jesus would act. Jesus had a charge; He wanted people to know the goodness of His Father. He could not deter His mission with the temporary feeling of drunkenness, instead Jesus found Himself indulged in prayer and teaching, reaching the people with the Good News of who He is and who God is. Can you do that drunk?

WHO CAN FIND A VIRTUOUS WOMAN???!!!! The Word speaks for itself, depicting strong characteristics, wisdom, skill, and compassion of a woman. The strength and dignity of this woman is not from her talents or achievements, but that of her reverence for God. Verses 1-9 speak of fearing the Lord; Verses 10-31 describes a virtuous woman and her qualities that exemplify worth, honor, success, and enjoyment. Furthermore, we can see the importance of our role with our families, our surroundings, and how our actions contribute to the well-being and quality of our lives. Psalm 139:14 tell us we are fearfully and wonderfully made. Therefore, we are an original masterpiece of the Creator, we are distinguished, and our worth is far more than jewels.

I challenge you to know yourself, your worth, and your God-given talents, skills, and gifts. Trust in the Lord with all thine heart and lean not on your own understanding; in all your ways acknowledge Him, and He shall direct your paths (Proverbs 3:5-6).

Peace and Blessings

3

From the Heart

For many are called but few are chosen. Matthew 22:14

Subsequent to walking through the Books of Psalms and Proverbs, I would reflect back on the writings and give God praise for using me. Without Him, I'm not sure how the blog or my prayer group would have turned out. Rereading the posts led me to freely write what came to heart and duplicate some of the posts for what was going on at the time.

The next set of writings are poems or poem-like writings that I shared in my blog and prayer group

From the Heart, Inspired by God...

What's In, Comes Out

Mark 7:20-23

"It is what comes from inside that defiles you. For from within, out of a person's heart, comes evil thoughts, sexual immorality, theft, murder, adultery, greed, wickedness, deceit, lustful desires, envy, slander, pride, and foolishness. All these vile things come from within; they are what defile you."

When we find ourselves characterized by one of these attributes, we must remember:

Philippians 4:8

"Fix your thoughts on what is true and honorable, and right, and pure, and lovely, and admirable. Think about things that are excellent and worthy of praise."

AND

Psalm 51:10

"Create in me a clean heart, O God; renew a loyal Spirit within me."

Examine your heart and emotions. Counteract the very thing that could be holding back your blessings or stifling your relationship with God.

New thoughts and desires.

Peace and Blessings

Change

Change can be defined as the transformation or conversion of what is, to something different. People sometimes convince themselves, "I just can't change. It's too late. Besides, I'm only human." They are not just belittling themselves; they are denying God's Word. They will fail simply because they will give up instead of persisting to use God's Power. Proverbs 4:23 - "Keep your heart with all diligence, for out of it are the issues of life." The way we act is determined by our attitudes and intentions. In this instance, we should not tangle with change as a grudge or issue but as a positive transformation that will benefit us in the long run. If the change does not exhibit beneficial transformation, then there is always a lesson to be learned, and we can begin to recognize what not to do. So don't get yourself in a tizzy, be open-minded to change, allow yourself to see other perspectives through change. God changed you when you were in the world and now you believe. Are you fighting for that change?

#pointtoponder

Peace and Blessings

As A Thriving Olive Tree

Olives trees are one of the oldest existing trees. They are usually planted close to streams or bodies of water. Olive trees have been known to live for 200 to 2,000 years and are fruitful trees. Olive trees only seem to be destroyed when not planted close to water or destroyed by man.

The olive tree also produces the fruit we call olive. Olives have some health and nutritional benefits and are symbolic in nature. The olive or olive leaves have been known to represent peace, wisdom, glory, fertility, power, and purity.

As trees are out in the elements, they are more susceptible to wear and tear, the threat of being chopped down, drying out from the lack of water or may not produce fruit.

As we have been enlightened about the olive tree, shouldn't we try to be more like olive trees? If we are planted in God's Word, always close and feeding from the Living Water - our very being is thriving to be more fruitful. Fruitful in the way we walk, fruitful in the way we talk, and fruitful within our spiritual connection. In addition, our thriving will begin to exhibit peace because we know God; wisdom because we read God's Word; glory because He gives us brand new grace and mercy every day, fertility because we can birth new beginnings and repent our sins, power because there is strength and victory when we accepted Christ, and purity because we believe Jesus can wash us white as snow.

As followers of Jesus and as a part of life, we are susceptible to trials and tribulations, the threat of falling short, separation from God, and not being able to share or spread the Good News. HOWEVER, when we stand firm in God's Word and withstand the wear and tear of this world, we continue to grow strong and fruitful. Are you thriving as an olive tree?

Peace and Blessings

The WISE Are
Mightier & Strong

Trials and tribulations can be useful. They can show us who we really are and what kind of character we have. We are to overcome trials and tribulations through wisdom. Just because we have endured and pressed through many previous trials and tribulations does not make us wise UNLESS we have learned from those previous trials and tribulations.

Once we have identified and adhered to the lessons learned, then we become STRONG in our decisions, thoughts, and actions. We must pray fervently to maintain and exercise our composure, thoughts, decisions, and how to appropriately handle any situation. Oh and those evildoers, don't fret - they have no future. God alone is the judge for their behaviors and gossip.

So before you lose your top, lash someone with your tongue, or find irritation setting in, STOP.

Remember the lessons you have learned, walk and talk like Jesus would - "Get you behind me, Satan: you are an offense unto me: for you consider not the things that be of God, but those that be of men" (Matthew 16:23). HA! and be on your merry way! Wisdom makes you strong.

Peace and Blessings

Do Not Be Drunk

We know the Bible tells us not to be drunk with wine, in addition to wine, do not be drunk with worldly ways. As believers, we must strive to stay aligned with God's Word and to continually pray and fight the battle. When we operate in the "world," our Christ-like senses are dulled, our judgment becomes limited, we become controlled by the flesh, and our efficiency becomes tainted.

The trials of the world can slowly but surely deteriorate our very being. The soul is thirsty, and we try to quench that thirst with many things that satisfy for a while, but eventually we get thirsty again. The only thing that can truly quench the thirst of the Spirit is the Living Water - Jesus Christ.

Jesus is the water needed by the spiritual aspect of man. Without Him, the soul will eventually die. So, do not be drunk with the things of this world, but choose Living Water and by drinking Living Water, one can live and never thirst again.

Thirst for Jesus.

Peace and Blessings

Priceless Value

In life, we go through things that are disheartening and discouraging, especially when it happens within our families.

Sometimes we and our family members stray from the Will of God. We may even become possessed with worldly ways.

Jesus cast out demons (worldly ways), and they went into pigs. Those pigs plunged off a cliff and drowned. We have the same power. We can tell those demons (worldly ways) that they can't have

us or our families and denounce their very being. We can take hold of our faith in God and move mountains. We can set the tone with the words we pray. We can find peace when we trust and believe. There is priceless value in trusting and believing. Isaiah 30:19 says, "how gracious He will be when you cry out for help!" We cry out to God for help, because we trust and believe.

Peace and Blessings

Where To Find Happiness

Do you truly know WHO you are? Day in and day out we run through life making sure we get to work/school on time; make it to meetings; make it to Bible study; cook dinner; do household chores; tend to the kids; try to have a social life; a few hours' sleep, and then it starts all over.

Reread that. Yup, no "me" time. At times we struggle because we don't know WHO we are. Can you answer the following questions without hesitation?

What makes you happy?

Are you happy?

What is happiness?

You had to think about it didn't you? Well, in order to get the fullness out of life, you must become intimate with yourself to recognize your desires, needs, and wants. In this, your desires, needs, and wants must warrant the Will of God and what He has for you. Drawing closer to God helps us understand who we are and in Him. God desires, needs, and wants us to seek Him in everything that we do, think, and speak. He desires, needs, and wants our attention, love, and devotion.

Look back over your daily schedule and make sure God is in every aspect; ensure you are doing your part in God's Will for you. If God is for us, who could be against us? Line up with God to get your happiness.

Peace and Blessings

Lemons

You know the phrase, "If life gives you lemons, make lemonade." Well let's rephrase that. "When

you receive Jesus, all things are possible!"

Lemons have many benefits; you can use them for health benefits (rich in Vitamin C, potassium, and magnesium), household chores (lemon juice and water are great grease cutters without the toxins), beauty aid (lemons whiten nails, rids dandruff, and gets rid of whiteheads), and other beneficial uses. On the other hand, a lemon can be bitter.

Just as lemons are universal and have many benefits, Jesus can heal the sick, cleanse your temple, remind you that you are wonderfully and beautifully made, and many other wonders and miracles. He also allows tests and trials.

To understand the beneficial use of lemons, you must gain knowledge of the uses besides dropping one in your tea. As for Jesus, He is the author of benefits and blessings in life. We must study God's Word to show ourselves approved, even through the bitter times.

Moral: Don't take for granted what you THINK you know. Study God's Word to SHOW what you KNOW!

Peace and Blessings

Mornting!

I'm up this morning with a grin on my face. I had an awesome visit with a friend last night. We talked a little bit about everything. We were able to share in the love, grace, and mercy that God has shown us through our daily lives and those close to us.

This reminded me that godly and supportive friendships provides a lifestyle of caring, giving, and receiving to include wisdom and edification that builds love and commitment. Words of patience, love, and wisdom are shared in the bond, a meeting of the minds - challenging and stimulating, and living in good company is beneficial.

Two or more are stronger than one, surround yourself with Godly friends, they have your best interests at heart. Remember that iron sharpens iron. He who walks with wise men will be wise (Proverbs 13:20).

Peace and Blessings

Good Night Thoughts

Now I lay me down to sleep, I pray the Lord my soul to keep. If I should die before I wake, I pray the Lord my soul to take.

Let's ponder.

More than likely, this prayer is one of the first we've learned and the most remembered. Learn and remember. *Learn* to gain or acquire knowledge. *Remember* to bring to one's mind. In life we learn and remember. As we grow in life we must remember what we've learned. In remembering we must also be wise. Being wise or having wisdom comes from God and His Word.

Moral: We must REMEMBER what we have LEARNED from WISDOM.

Commune with God! He would love to hear from you!

Peace and Blessings

As We Prepare

Today is the day that the Lord has made, let us rejoice and be glad in it. These words are familiar, but are you living it? Tests and trials come daily. Expect them. The key is to know what battle you're fighting and how to fight it. So if today poses any tests or trials, know that it is a SPIRITUAL BATTLE, and we fight with THE WORD. God will never put much more on us than we can bear, so today is the day that we change our attitude, commune with God, build a relationship with Him that keeps us coming back for more. Know that He is the head and should be consulted first in all decisions that we make.

This is the day, when we are no longer harassed with those things which vex us in the worldliness of the day. A day when we think of God, of redemption, of hope, and of Heaven. When we think on these things, it strengthens, refreshes, and consoles the heart from burdens and sorrowful times, and it lifts the soul to a joyous state of being where wearisome toll and sorrow shall be no more. Read your Word, be encouraged, and fight any and all battles with His Word!

Peace and Blessings

The Days Of Our Lives

The days of our lives are numbered and only God knows the end. Before our day has come, we have been commissioned to follow and do the greater work of God's Word. We must be strong enough to tread through the wilderness. We must be wise in decision-making and give glory to God in every aspect of our being. Live life for God, live life that you should receive eternal life. Do not slumber, rely only on the strength that God supplies and live in His Word for the rest of the days of your life.

Peace and Blessings

Press & Prize

Some days are more stressful than others, some days even seem to only bring about problems. Instead of giving into the stress and issues life throws at us, we must keep pressing! Philippians 3:14 states, "I press on to reach the end of the race and receive the heavenly prize for which God, through Christ Jesus, is calling us" (NLT). So when you are feeling overwhelmed, remember to press (press -move or to push through) past stress and issues, remember the prize (eternal life) you will receive when you continue to follow Jesus.

Question to ponder: is the prize worth pressing?

Peace and Blessings

Turning Over A New Leaf

Therefore if anyone is in Christ, he is a new creation; the old has gone and the new has come! (II Corinthians 5:17). Amen! If you are in Christ you must remember that the OLD is gone and the NEW is here. When we adhere to God's Word and begin to live accordingly, we are turning over a new leaf. Turning means to change or convert. A new leaf is the next page in the chapter of your life. The pages of our lives must be turned to get the rest of the story. If we stay on the same page we will keep doing and reading the same thing over and over, but when we turn a new leaf we move on to the next phase of our being. We must not forget what our past story is or where we came from,

but we must move forward in godly growth and press for the mark. Do not be stagnant in your old ways but allow God's grace and mercy to encourage your journey forward with no fears, doubts, or complaints. Turn from the very things that have you bound and will not allow you to flourish; turn away from negative aspects that drown your spirit; turn to God in who all things are possible.

Are you turning a new leaf?

Peace and Blessings

We Never Stop Learning...

As children of God, we get many of our teachings from the Book of Proverbs. The purpose of Proverbs is to teach people how to attain wisdom, discipline, and how to live right, just, and fair. The teachings in Proverbs address family life, self-control, resisting temptations, business matters, marriage, knowing God, seeking the truth, wealth, poverty, immorality, and wisdom (just to name a few).

A little history - Proverbs is a Hebrew word for "to rule or to govern." Therefore, God has provided us with the rules to govern our lives. We must adhere to what the Book of Proverbs can teach us and put those teachings into learned behaviors. When we have learned these teachings, our learned behaviors will exhibit strong characteristics that include wisdom, relationship building, a good attitude, hard work, and successful living. Learn what God has provided for us in Proverbs and discover the source, value, and benefits of Godly living.

Peace and Blessings

Private Deliverance Deserves Public Testimony

When we are battling decisions, hurting, or have confusion, we can go to God in prayer. We can even get intimate with Him and cry out in our own personal closet. In our closet, we confess, snot, cry, pour out emotions, speak life, seek comfort, and when God sees fit, we get delivered. Delivered from the things that had us upset, bound, off track, wavering, or what has separated us from the love of God.

God honors His relationship with His children and will be in the midst when we call on Him. God will pick us up and give us answers to problems and when we have come through a battle...we must let others know that the victory was won. We must give God His props when He brings us through, when He allows the desires of our hearts, when He makes changes for our better, when He has given us the answer to our prayers, and when He allows us to see things come to pass. These things are testimonies.

A testimony is evidence or truth from a witness. When we have testimonies, we can encourage someone else or let them see how God works. We can provide insight to a battle someone is going through that we may have already been through and were victorious in the end. We are not to be ashamed or embarrassed, but willing to speak boldly about our experiences and give God the glory for the outcomes.

With God, we can be delivered from anything, and when we are delivered, we can let others know how great our God is through our testimony.

Yes Lord!

Peace and Blessings

Get Right!

Proverbs 28:9 tell us if one turns his ear from hearing the law of God, even his prayer shall be an abomination. In light of this scripture, are you abiding by God's Word? Do you wonder if God is hearing your prayers? Should God turn a deaf ear to your prayers when you have denied reading, studying, and putting action to His Word?

In every relationship there is a role. We must know our role in our relationship with God. God has called us as His chosen people and as His chosen people, we must abide by His laws and commands that are written for us in His Word. When we are aligned and have a real relationship with God, He will hear our prayers. However, Isaiah 59:2 states: when your iniquities or sinfulness has separated you from God, your sins have hidden His face from you so that He will not hear you.

Ponder your relationship with God and make improvements in areas you lack. Keep your relationship on track and allow God to do what He said He would do. God will keep the promises of His covenant, and we will dwell in the house of the Lord forever!

Have a relationship with God.

Peace and Blessings

We Are Blessed!

We experience blessings from the Lord when we obey Him and carefully keep His commands. He will set us above all the nations, and we will be blessed in the city, blessed in the fields, our children will be blessed, where ever we go, whatever we do, we are blessed. (Deuteronomy 28:1-6). We are cursed when we refuse to listen to the Lord and do not obey His commands; the curses will come and be overwhelming; we will be cursed in the city, cursed in the fields, curse our children, wherever we go, whatever we do, we will be cursed (Deuteronomy 28:15-19).

Make a choice: Blessed or Cursed? Scriptures to ponder.

Peace and Blessings

Speak Life

Life is full of ups and downs. Sometimes we feel empty and other times we may feel overwhelmed. Feeling empty can be a result of disconnect from God, emotional strain, stress, or the unknown. During these times, we have the privilege and honor to seek God in prayer to handle our discontentment.

God is the ultimate listener and gives us wisdom to speak life over our situations. Feeling overwhelmed can be a result of disconnect from God, not using good judgment, or getting caught up in selfish or worldly ways. Again, we have the privilege and honor to seek God in prayer to handle our discontentment.

God knows everything about you, even before you were in the womb; so why not consult with the Creator? To consult with the Creator takes effort on your part. He is always ready and willing to hear and take care of His own, but you must keep God first, as the head of your life. You must communicate with God on a regular and daily basis to seek an understanding of how to counteract the very emotions that draw on your well-being and happiness.

God's Word can fill empty voids. God's Word can surpass overwhelming situations. God can! So when there are a rush of misunderstood emotions such as emptiness or being overwhelmed, exercise your ability to seek and speak to God. Remember that your Heavenly Father is all powerful and when you seek Him in all that you do and experience, the ultimate outcome is Heavenly.

Peace and Blessings

Trust

Trust can be described as a firm belief or strength regarding the relationship of a person or situation. We learn trust through responsibility, bonding, and risk-taking. In life, our parents taught us the significance of knowing God, how to budget money, and how to take care of ourselves - these responsibilities have built "trust;" in what we have learned and how we relate to different aspects.

We create relationships where we grow close to others and share intimate information and time spent - and over a period of time, we begin to trust or get comfortable with the other in the relationship or bond. As risk-takers, when we believe something, we are not afraid to face tasks or issues head-on because we have faith in God's Will for the outcome; and faith builds trust.

Collectively, trust describes how we should be with God. He has given us responsibility to learn lessons from His Word and live according to His Word. We must communicate with Him every day to build the relationship or bond that draws us closer to Him; we must have faith that all we do in our decision-making and actions are lined up with the Will of God. When we are lined up, we are able to face risks or issues head-on because we TRUST what we have

learned from His Word and know He would never leave nor forsake us.

Examine your heart today. Do you have trust issues? Go to God and ask Him to give you clarity. Ask Him to show you how to trust in His Word. Learn your responsibility in your spiritual walk, bond with God and His Word so that you become familiar and equipped with scriptures for battle; and get grounded in the Word so that when it's time to step out on faith, you know that you can rely on God to see you through. Find trust in the Lord, then everything else will fall into place. (*Repost from Psalm 101*).

Peace and Blessings

Meet Grace And Mercy

I want to introduce you to Grace and Mercy. Grace is God's free and unmerited favor toward sinful humanity and Mercy is a blessing of favor or compassion from God. Now that you have met them, can you see the connection? Wait for it...FAVOR!

God's grace is His favor of mercy to forgive a person's sins. God renews grace and mercy every day! Repent your sins, align with God's Word and receive your Favor!

Grace+Mercy=Favor

Peace and Blessings

SINGING!!!!!!

When we all get to Heaven. What a day of rejoicing that will be! When we all see Jesus. We will sing and shout the VICTORY!

When there is a song on your heart, let Jesus hear it, He loves to hear the praises of His name!

Peace and blessings

A Fast Strategy

We are what we eat, this is one of the reasons why we should cleanse our bodies. The goal is to get rid of all the toxins in our bodies and to eat healthier. At the same time, we are feeding our minds. In an effort to cleanse our minds of toxins, we should read God's Word and inspirational readings daily. In addition, we can also engage in alternatives to fasting. The following is an example of a four week alternative fast:

Week 1 - Abstain from secular music. Listen to spiritual or gospel music only.

Week 2 - Abstain from over spending or unnecessary purchases. Use this week to get your finances in order.

Week 3 - Abstain from TV and all social media platforms.

Week 4 - Abstain from negative outburst, arguing, tellin' folks off, gossiping, etc.

Be encouraged to pray, read, and study during your alternative fasting. Additional ideas to replace the void: do some soul searching, exercise, stay current with your eating/reading plans, visit with the sick/shut-in, visit with family members, volunteer at a community function, define goals for yourself, organize your house, clean your car inside and out, plan quality time with your children, journal, study issues or topics that interest you, go to the library, research/make recipes, schedule overdue appointments with doctors, remind yourself that you are fearfully and wonderfully made, and that all things are possible when we align with God's Word.

Peace and Blessings

Denying The Flesh

To deny the flesh of its natural desires may allow us to be more "in tune" to hear the voice of the Lord, but it also places us in a realm more easily prone to the attack of the enemy. When Jesus was fasting for forty days, He was faced with the greatest of Satanic attacks (Matthew 4:1-3; Luke 4:1-2).

The devil is aware of our fasting (fasting should be done in humility and secrecy - Matthew 6:16-18). He focuses on tempting us in the very areas or reasoning for our fasting. The devil often tempts us when we are vulnerable, i.e. when we are physically and emotionally stressed, lonely, tired, weighing big decisions, or faced with

uncertainty. We must guard against the devil at all times and resist temptations by not only knowing scripture but obeying it.

As you journey through your fast, remember to guard yourself, don't deny reading God's Word. Don't deny DAILY communication with God. Learn and memorize scripture and put action to what you've learned about scripture. Lastly, don't make your fast a trial. Your fasting is what God desires - your drawing closer to Him, learning Him, knowing Him, and striving to be like Him.

Peace and Blessings

Deny Ourselves

When we have trouble maintaining consistency in our devotion to God, it is usually because it does not come naturally to deny ourselves and put God and His interests ahead of our own. A regular practice of fasting and prayer helps assure more consistency in our devotion to God because it develops a lifestyle of self-denial. This part of fasting is true discipleship.

Jesus said, "If anyone would come after me, he must deny himself and take up his cross daily and follow me" Luke 9:23.

Peace and Blessings

Addictions

When we speak of addiction, most want to assume that addictions only deal with drugs, drinking, or sexual acts. However, this does not hold true. One can be addicted to salt, sugar, TV, and even feeling emotional desires. Addictions can be powerful and hard to break; in this instance, we must discover the root of our addictions.

Addictions are created through desires that inadvertently become a regular habit or dependency. Desires are thoughts and/or emotions that manifest into actions or behaviors. If we want to change the desires of our addictions, we must pray and fast.

How we respond to the change in addiction can be healthy or unhealthy. To make healthy changes we must consider positive actions or behaviors, like taking a walk, deep breathing, or thinking faith-filled thoughts. We do this in place of worrying, nail biting, or continuing with the addiction. II Peter 2:18-19 states, "for a man is a slave to whatever has mastered him." We must not be slaves to addictions or what has mastered us, but we must fast and pray to set our minds on resisting the addiction. We must stand firm in God's Word as our guide to weaken the power of addiction and gain back our self-control.

As we are soldiers in God's army, we must use our battle tactics to bring our minds and bodies under submission and take control. We beat down those very things that have us bound, we do not rely on what addiction says we need. God supplies ALL of our needs, and a soldier without worldly needs cannot be tempted and will not turn from duty.

Now tell yourself, I am a soldier in God's army. There is no addiction that can harm me, for I fight my battles with scripture, prayer, and fasting (in our MLK voice we tell those addictions) FREE AT LAST, FREE AT LAST, THANK GOD ALMIGHTY I AM FREE AT LAST!

Peace and Blessings

Spreading The Good News

God has charged us to get to know Him and to spread the Good News. How do we get to know God and how do we spread the Good News? To know God we must read, study, and fellowship. Reading the Bible gives us insight to God's instruction for our lives. Studying the Bible allows us to learn God's character, desires, and truth about our very being. When we fellowship, we should fellowship with like kind or with those of the same yolk who share in the same beliefs and to encourage one another. When we deny reading, studying, and fellowship with like kind - we are denying God.

To spread the Good News about Jesus Christ, we must be prepared when faced with situations when we should witness, give spiritual guidance, or speak existence of God's Word to others. We are not to let any wind of doctrine toss us to and fro (Ephesians 4:14), but to stand firm on what we know about scripture and inform others of our knowledge and experiences

with God. We must take control of how we learn about God. We become wise in our daily decisions and have dominion over our trials and tribulations when we are in tune with His Word.

When we read, study, and fellowship on a regular basis, our persons will shine with God's light. When we have neglected to read, study, and fellowship, we tend to fish around with what we know on the surface and begin to bring in our own thoughts and ways. Half doing work for God will only get you half way down the road to Heaven; and denying God His time will only get you a knock on the door and when answered, you'll be asked "Who are you?"

God is all-powerful, wonderful, an awesome provider, omnipotent, and gracious; yet some of us continue through our daily lives without giving reverence to Him. We can show reverence through our obedience, reading, studying, and fellowship. Stop making God and His desires second to your selfish ways, allow time to do what He asks of you, prove to GOD that you trust and have real faith in Him. Stop running off at the mouth, whooping it up in your social life and begin to come into His image. Run and tell somebody about Jesus and commune with your church family or like kind.

Peace and Blessings

Good Stewards

We must learn to be good stewards over our money. Organizing our daily lives can decrease frustrations and increase our preparedness for unforeseen situations. In our organizing, we must budget our finances and budgeting our finances is merely knowing what is coming in and what is going out. We must create a plan to keep us out of debt such as paying off credit cards, starting an emergency fund, decreasing expenses, bargain shopping, categorizing expenses, and tracking in and outgoing monies. Proverbs 21:5 states that good planning and hard work lead to prosperity, but hasty shortcuts lead to poverty (NLT).

Part of living abundantly involves planning and preparing that includes budgeting and saving.

Budgeting is your plan to have structure to your income and your outgoing expenses. We must learn to keep these transactions in perspective and in order to live comfortably within our means. When we live within our means, we also should keep our future in mind by saving. Saving is the resources or reserves that we should diligently set aside for a rainy day. Learning to regularly put some of our income aside will provide a cushion for those unexpected expenses or situations.

Collectively, we must have self-discipline to have control over our finances and not allow debt or out of control expenses or spending take root in how we manage our money. When we have self-discipline over our finances, we are more stable to make required or desired purchases, payments, or to get out of debt. Proverbs 24:27 tells us "do your planning and prepare your fields before building your house" (NLT). In other words, budget and save before making major financial decisions.

Peace and Blessings

Defining Prayer

Prayer can be defined as a solemn request for God's assistance, expression of thanks toward God, or means of worship. Prayer is essential for our spiritual being and communication with God. The Bible tells us to pray without ceasing (I Thessalonians 5:17), this means to continually have prayer in our mouths. Through every aspect of our day or interactions, we should be praying; with every thought, we should be praying.

Prayer is not a specific action that requires closed eyes, kneeling, or being anointed with oil. Prayer is our regular, active communication, thanks, or worship to God that can take place anywhere, any time.

Today I encourage you to study "prayer". Know the importance of prayer and what it means in your spiritual walk.

Peace and Blessings

Watch Your Mouth

Colossians 3:8

But now you must put them all away: anger, wrath, malice, slander, and obscene talk from your mouth.

Proverbs 21:23

Whoever keeps his mouth, and his tongue keeps himself out of trouble.

Although the tongue is one of our smallest body parts, it is one of the strongest. What we speak reveals our thoughts and feelings.

Every word we speak should be "gracious" and "seasoned with salt" (Colossians 4:6).

We should always ask, "What would Jesus say?"

Point to Ponder: It only takes a spark to start a forest fire. The tongue is like a spark.

Peace and Blessings

Phases

Just as seasons change, we go through phases of life. These phases come with ups and downs; when good times are high - we tend to live comfortably with no worries; when times are not so good- we tend to slump and complain. HOWEVER, we can live in peace through it all.

Philippians 4:6-7

Don't worry about anything; instead, pray about everything.

Tell God what you need and thank Him for all He has done. Then you will experience God's peace, which exceeds anything we can understand. His peace will guard your heart and mind as you live in Christ Jesus.

Read this scripture several times and let it sink in. Don't worry, pray, communicate, praise, and experience peace. These are the key aspects I picked up reading this scripture.

Thinking back over things that worry me, I choose to pray, communicate with God, give Him praise for keeping me, experience His peace by allowing Him to lead me, and trust that God has my heart and mind guarded as I walk with Christ.

Apply this scripture to your situations. Let go and let God!

Peace and Blessings

Rejoice!

Philippians 4:4

Rejoice in the Lord always; and again I say, Rejoice!

Every day is a day to rejoice. The goodness of Jesus is enough to keep us rejoicing yesterday, today, tomorrow, and forever.

Reflect over what Jesus has done for you and how He keeps you. Encourage someone today, let them know that joy comes every morning, whatever the situation, we are covered by His grace and mercy. No matter what, Jesus is always with us! Hallelujah and Amen!

Peace and Blessings

Rooted

Ephesians 3:17

Then Christ will make His home in your hearts as you trust in Him. Your roots will grow down into God's love and keep you strong.

Faith is trust in God, and the only way to develop faith is to learn and know God.

Functions of roots are imperative to our survival. Like the roots of a tree, they anchor the tree to provide stability. Our reading and praying serve as roots so that we are anchored in God's Word and communication. Roots take in water to supply nourishment and encourages growth - Jesus is Living Water that brings forth life and quenches thirst. Roots also store the water and minerals in its trunk - God's Word is in us. When in need we can rely on what we know about God and His Word.

I trust Him, I know Him, and I am rooted in Him. Thank you Jesus for saving ME!!!!!

Peace and Blessings

Renewed & Clean

We are born into sin, and this causes the flesh or our natural being to follow worldly desires. Asking God to cleanse us from these very things and filling us with new thoughts and desires that are reflective of Him will influences right conduct. Right conduct can only come from a clean heart and spirit. If you

are experiencing setbacks and indecisiveness, meet God in your secret closet, pray and commune, ask God for clarity, understanding, wisdom, and a clean heart. As Fred Hammond sings "Give me a clean heart and I will serve nobody but You!"

Keep seeking God, press to be more like Him, and watch how He blesses you.

Peace and Blessings

Faithful & Honest

Luke 16:10

If you are faithful in little things, you will be faithful in large ones. But if you are dishonest in little things, you will be dishonest with greater responsibilities.

Big or small, we must remain faithful. We must also learn to be honest in everything we do even when it's not how we would want it to be, or we disagree. Honesty is the best policy. Try it.

Peace and Blessings

Veil Removed

II Corinthians 3:18

So all of us who have had that veil removed can see and reflect on the glory of the Lord. And the Lord, who is the Spirit, makes us more and more like Him as we are changed into His glorious image.

Verse 16 of the same book and chapter states, but whenever someone turns to the Lord, the veil is taken away. This means that we no longer have on blinders to what we know about God and His Word. Some of us were experiencing the "veiling" of the mind or burdens, a hardened heart, or pride. When we give our heart and mind to God FIRST, the "veil" is removed or you begin to understand and abide by God's Word; you realize that all things are possible with God, and you commune with Him in all that you do; you forgive and pray; you live according to God's Will and what He has for YOU.

Gain eternal life by accepting Christ, become free from bondage by living His Word, THEN you will begin to reflect God's Glory!

Peace and Blessings

The Scales

John 10:10

The thief's purpose is to steal, kill and destroy. My purpose is to give them a rich and satisfying life.

God has given us a choice; we can continue to sin and not align with God and His Word that ultimately leads to destruction, or we can choose God and get aligned with His Word and receive abundant living and eternal life. Weigh the options, the scales should not be unbalanced. Does your scale lean more toward thieves or Jesus?

Peace and Blessings

Living

Hebrews 12:14

Work at living in peace with everyone, and work at living a holy life, for those who are not holy will not see the Lord.

Sin always blocks our relationship with God and if we want to see Him, we must renounce sin and obey Him. Holiness is relative to living in peace and we must be holy or clean to be in a right relationship with God. A right relationship with God leads to right relationships with fellow believers and others. Although we may not always feel loving toward fellow believers or others, we must pursue peace as we become more Christ-like. WE have a responsibility to live upright IF we are living for Christ.

Peace and Blessings

Let It Go!

Mark 11:25

But when you are praying, first forgive anyone you are holding a grudge against, so that your Father in Heaven will forgive your sins, too.

A person praying while bearing a grudge is like a tree sprouting leaves and bearing no fruit. We must pray with fervent effort to dismantle any grudges or vengeance. We must remove pride, use real faith and lose the hurt and grudges and begin to forgive. In all we do, pray God's Will.

Peace and Blessings

Remain Strong

Isaiah 40:31

But those who trust in the Lord will find new strength. They will soar high on wings like eagles. They will run and not get weary.

Trusting in the Lord is the patient expectation that God will fulfill His promises and strengthen us to rise above any difficulties. We must remain confident in God that He has all control and that He would never leave nor forsake us. Stop complaining and worrying and know that God is! We must begin to show God that we DO trust Him and that our very being, actions, and thoughts are that of His.

Renew yourself in God and remain one of His strong soldiers!

Peace and Blessings

Commit

Colossians 2:6-7

And now, just as you accepted Christ Jesus as your Lord, you must continue to follow Him. Let our roots grow down into Him, and let your lives be built on Him.

Then your faith will grow strong in the truth you were taught, and you will overflow with thankfulness.

We must be built up, rooted, and strengthened in the Lord. We must commit and submit to Him and Him only. We must seek to learn from Him, His life, and His teachings. We must recognize Him in us. We will be overjoyed when we put Him first and live our lives accordingly.

Peace and Blessings

At Peace

II Timothy 1:7 (NLT)

For God has not given us a spirit of fear and timidity, but of power, love, and self-discipline.

God has given us the Holy Spirit to help us overcome any adversities. He has also given us love or strong affection, power or the ability to influence, and self-discipline (sound mind) or control of our behaviors and thoughts. Collectively, we have the tools to live in peace and to be faithful unto God.

Peace and Blessings

Limits

Galatians 1:10

Obviously, I'm not trying to win the approval of people, but of God. If pleasing people were my goal, I would not be Christ's servant.

We must know our limits when assisting, helping, or giving our time to others. We must ensure that we give God an ample amount of our time in regard to communing with Him, praying to Him, reading His Word, and behaving Christ-like. We serve a God that loves attention, and we must seek His approval, not that of the flesh or others. PERIOD.

Peace and Blessings

White As Snow

Isaiah 1:18 (NLT)

"Come now, let's settle this," says the Lord. "Though your sins are like scarlet, I will make them as white as snow. Though they are red like crimson, I will make them as white as wool."

Crimson is a color of deep red permanent color, and its deep stain is virtually impossible to get out of clothing. Stains of sin are equally permanent. However, God can remove sin stains and make us clean. Stop using that Tide pen whereas the stain is still there and visible. Repent and ask God to wash you white as snow!

Peace and Blessings

Obedient

I Peter 1:2

God the Father knew you and chose you long ago, and His Spirit has made you holy. As a result, you have obeyed Him and have been cleansed by the blood of Jesus Christ. May God give you more and more grace and peace.

Our Father rewards us for our obedience, continue to stay on His righteous path and receive grace, peace, abundance, and joy.

Peace and Blessings

In Motion

James 5:16 (NLT)

The prayer of a righteous man is powerful and effective.

Did you grasp that? Every time you pray, you set something in motion. Every time you pray, something in the universe changes. You have never wasted a prayer in your life. Not one falls through the cracks. Your prayer life makes you powerful and effective for God's work and your needs. Whether you speak your prayer out loud, sing it, whisper it, or just think it in your head. God hears you!

Peace and Blessings

Kept!

I Peter 1:8 (NLT)

You love Him even though you have never seen Him. Though you do not see Him now, you trust Him; and you rejoice with a glorious, inexpressible joy.

God has been so good to me and my family. Through the ups and downs, He STILL has kept us, even when I felt like I was at my lowest and issues were and are coming against my family members. God STILL covers us. No matter what may come my way, I choose to fight the battle with God's Word. Therefore, I rebuke any snares or weapons formed against me, my family, friends, and enemies; I stand firm in my FAITH knowing that God has full control and NOTHING shall separate me from my God. Declare life and joy today! For you and your family, speak life and peace into all situations, dare to be bold in Christ Jesus. We serve an awesome God and He deserves all of our praise!!!!

Peace and Blessings

New Man

Ephesians 4:22-24

Throw off your old sinful nature and your former way of life, which is corrupted by lust and deception. Instead, let the spirit renew your thoughts and attitudes. Put on your new nature, created to be like God, truly righteous and holy.

How can you do this?

II Timothy 3:16-17 (NLT) All scripture is inspired by God and is useful to teach us what is true and to make us realize what is wrong in our lives. It corrects us when we are wrong and teaches us to do what is right. God uses it to prepare and equip His people to do every good work.

When faced with daily challenges, big or small, we MUST always rely on God's guidance to see us through. READ GOD'S WORD DAILY. In addition, we MUST pray without ceasing and speak life into the situations we are faced with...although the situations may not change overnight, we MUST remain strong in our faith that good will come and that anything formed against us shall not prosper. Work hard to do good, live right, obey God's commands, and line up with His Word. Face every waking minute like it's your last, seek the Kingdom of Heaven, ask God to renew your mind, attitude, behaviors, what you speak, how you speak, when to speak, and how to overcome. Speak to yourself, identify your flaws, work to relinquish all things that are not of God, REPENT, and live abundantly. Your God, my God, our God can do all things possible, so why weep and complain when we already have the victory, we MUST learn to claim what God has for us and LEARN to line up and follow through.

ACTIONS enhance the words we speak. Now ask yourself - Am I living as a dead man that is supposed to be passed away, or am I pressing to live like the new man God has allowed me to be?

Be diligent in praying over your children and their daily lives and activities; pray over your finances, relationships, our government, our work places, our friends and enemies, and pray that God will use you in a way that you are beneficial and will bring glory to Him.

I can't express enough how imperative our prayer life is, and how God seeks us INDIVIDUALLY and wants to hear and commune with us! Although we all fall short of the glory of God, this does not give us a free pass to be an _ _ _!

Wake up! Get up! Make our Father proud! Let's get it church!

Peace and Blessings

Tired?

Matthew 11:28 (NLT)

Then Jesus said, "Come to me, all of you who are weary and carry heavy burdens, and I will give you rest."

Read this scripture several times to get the full meaning of it. JESUS SAID (know who is talking), ALL who are WEARY AND CARRY HEAVY BURDENS - Come to me (He is giving instructions on what to do when you're going through) - then He said - I will give you rest. Not you, yourself, but Jesus. He will give you rest or relief. So many times we try to handle things in our own strength, but our strength is not always sufficient like Jesus. We must learn to PRAY and give our weariness and burdens over to Him (we give it over by reading and knowing His Word and applying the Word to life and our life situations). We must learn that even when we give things over to Him that we must be patient and watch how He unfolds the outcome and stop complaining and wanting a microwave minute outcome.

If you have gotten off track with your relationship with God and your reading is at a standstill, how do you think God feels when you come begging for answers and outcomes? We must do our part in the relationship and stop acting like we have not fallen short.

Commune with God daily, read your Word daily and let it seep into your soul, repent your old ways and let the new man grow. You are no longer on breast milk but table food. Stand firm on what you believe in and do not let the wiles of the world get you down, instead be a soldier in God's army. For God so loved the world that He gave His only begotten Son (could you?).

Respect who is all powerful, almighty, all giving, omnipresent, and to whom all you can ask or think. No more pity parties, no more complaining, no more trying in your own strength. Give God what He is due - your attention, time, and obedience.

Father God, I thank You this morning for speaking to my heart, informing me that You have not left me nor forsaken me, letting me continue on the path of righteousness even though I have fallen short. Thank You for being a loving and graceful God. Thank You for waking us this morning. Thank You for giving us grace and mercy, Thank You for still allowing us to run back to Your arms when we have been distant. Thank You for hearing our cries when we pick and choose when to communicate with You. Thank You for giving us a manual to live by that will never steer us wrong. Thank You for allowing us to share in happiness and sadness that we may love, encourage and help one another, thank You that we have to look no further for the TRUTH and understanding. Although we may move slow You still said You will take the one over 99. God, You are so awesome, and I pray right now that You heal the sick, comfort the weary, encourage the lost, give light to the dark, provide for the obedient, give understanding to the misunderstood, take corruption out of our government and jobs, cover our families from all hurt, harm, and danger, give our children wisdom to follow Your guidance along with their parents. I thank

You God that You are who You say You are and that the answers to our prayers will come to fruition. I pray all of these things in Your precious Son's name, Jesus. We love and honor You and ask for forgiveness and repent those things that are not of You. Thank YOU Jesus, thank You Jesus, thank You Jesus. AMEN!!

Peace and Blessings

Saved!

Romans 10:9-11(NLT)

If you confess with your mouth that Jesus is Lord and believe in your heart that God raised Him from the dead, you will be saved. For it is by believing in your heart that you are made right with God, and it is by confessing with your mouth that you are saved. As the Scriptures tells us, "Anyone who trusts in Him will never be disgraced."

Ephesians 2:8-9 (NLT)

God saved you by His grace when you believed. And you can't take credit for this; it is a gift from God.

The experience of the Roman's Road is the gift of salvation and because our salvation is a gift, we should respond to God with gratitude, praise, and joy.

We must remember to give God what He longs for, our attention, worship, and praise. We get so caught up in our daily lives that we make little time or communication with the very one who gave us life here on earth and eternal life. When we pass away, we will not have the duty to go to work or school, to complain about bills, to be stressed about this or that, so while we are still here, we must show God and the world that we appreciate Him by being obedient to His Word, sharing in fellowship, encouraging others, living right, putting old ways behind us, confessing and repenting our sins, recognizing the power within us to avoid temptations, speak life into dying situations, assist the needy, love our families, raise our children in the way they should go, take pride in our spiritual walk, read and study His Word, give action to what we read in His Word, pray for the sick and shut-in; pray for our enemies, pray for those who have sheltered themselves from God, put on God's full body of armor daily, sing His praises, and give thanks no matter what.

The question is now posed. With so much to do with and for God, why do we have so little time for Him but have plenty of time for our worldly issues and day-to-day activities that we always seem to pray over?

Your prayer life could be much less complex if you prayed on a daily basis and strive to live according to His Word.

Father God I thank You for yet again Your grace and mercy. I confess with my mouth that Jesus is Lord, and I do believe You raised Him from the dead for my sins, I am honored and humbled that You have given me such a gift. I will strive to be more and more like You and give precedence to my spiritual learning and growing. I pray Father God that You prick the hearts of those reading this book, that they should find new life in their situations and families, that we learn to trust You with every word, actions, and of our being, that we may not only look to You in our time of need, but when things are going well. I pray that You bless each and every individual in the realm in which we struggle or are pulling through. I pray that our children call on You for guidance in their lives, that our prayer life become part of our everyday, that our schools, government, and jobs become tolerable and influential for our well-being, I pray for those that are less fortunate, I pray for those with sickness and ailments, I pray for the homeless and helpless, I pray for the atheists and racists, I pray for the corruption of this world, I pray for those who are dealing with the loss of loved ones, I pray for those that think they are hiding from You, I pray for the words we speak, I pray for the strength only You can provide, I pray for our pastors and first families, I pray for our churches, I pray for sound mind, and I praise You Lord for all You have done, continue to do and thank You for Your everlasting grace and mercy! Hear us today Lord. Change our lives, we want to draw closer to You! I pray all of these things in Your precious Son's name, Jesus! Amen!

Peace and Blessings

Help Mate

Ecclesiastes 4:9-10 (NLT)

Two people are better off than one, for they can help each other succeed. If one person falls, the other can reach out and help. But someone who falls alone is in real trouble.

God created Eve for Adam; this tells us that life was designed for companionship and intimacy. God does not desire for us to be alone or without love and trust in someone. So as brothers and sisters in Christ, we must learn to have prayerful relationships with our fellow like-minded (and others).

When one of us are struggling, we should be able to come together to pray and encourage one another, we should express our love and concern for one another, and we must become team players and assist each other while here on Earth. With Christian companionship, we learn to love, give, speak life, pray, encourage, help, and share in God's Will and Wisdom. Pray and encourage someone today, you never know how you may be a blessing to someone.

Peace and Blessings

Holy Spirit

Romans 15:13 (NLT)

I pray that God, the source of hope, will fill you completely with joy and peace because you trust in Him. Then you will overflow with confident hope through the power of the Holy Spirit.

As long as we continue to trust God, live according to His Word, and pray unceasingly, we can have joy and peace no matter what the day may bring. We must recognize when the Spirit is working in us and through us. God gave us a gift of a Comforter that is ALWAYS with us, therefore we have no need to fret or to relinquish to sin or temptation. Keep your mind and temple aligned with God's Word, feed your spirit with that of His righteousness, and press to make everyday a day that God receives His praise and joy from YOU.

Peace and Blessings

No Worries

I Peter 5:7

Give all your worries and cares to God, for He cares about you.

Carrying your struggles, stress, and worries by yourself shows that you do not fully trust God. Sometimes we think that our struggles, stress, and worries are caused by our sins and foolishness, regardless of where they stem from, when we REPENT and give them over to God, He will bear the weight for us. Don't submit to circumstances, submit to the Lord.

Peace and Blessings

You Know!

James 4:17 (NLT)

Remember, it is a sin to know what you ought to do and then not do it.

We often want to view sin as doing wrong, but sin can also be viewed as not doing right. It is a sin to lie, and it is also a sin to know the truth and not tell it. God has given us instructions to be kind, render services, help one another, encourage each other, and other instruction that influence a humble and loving personality. So we must take what we know about God's Word and put it into action through our walk and talk. Speak life over yourself, family, friends, and enemies. You never know what someone is going through and your words may be the very words to cover or comfort them.

Every day is a day of renewed blessings, grace, mercy, and joy, but we only experience these attributes when we actively live to receive them. To receive blessings, grace, mercy, and joy, we must be in touch with the one who gives them, God. Commune with Him daily, every day, all day. We must read and study His Word. The Bible tells us we must get the Word for ourselves to show ourselves approved. Are you approved? We must live according to what the Word teaches us; not just read it and "ping" a light bulb comes on after reading a verse. We must strive to live Christ-like, fight the spiritual battle and prove that YOU are victorious. God said it's already done, so we know the end. You must learn to press through any situation. Resist evil and he shall flee.

Peace and Blessings

Victory!

John 16:33

I have told you all this so that you may have peace in Me. Here on Earth you will have many trials and sorrows. But take heart, because I have overcome the World.

Up to this point in the scripture, Jesus spoke about vines and branches, warns of world hatred, teaches about using His name in prayer, that He himself prays, and other values. He revealed all of these things so that we may have peace, in spite of the things that may form against us, any trials or tribulations, or any struggles we endure. We must know in our hearts that Jesus died for us, and He has conquered the world and the things thereof. In this, we have peace, happiness, joy, and the victory.

Peace and Blessings

Blessed

John 14:1-3 (NLT)

Don't let your hearts be troubled. Trust in God, and trust also in Me. There is more than enough room in my Father's home. If this were not so, would I have told you that I am going to prepare a place for you? When everything is ready, I will come for you, so that you will always be with me where I am.

We are blessed! Jesus has paved the way for us to have eternal life, the only thing that could hold us back is the unwillingness to believe and not live what we believe.

Peace and Blessings

Such As Life

When we deal with issues of life, sometimes our first response is to complain, grumble, murmur, tell our family or friends, and how we wish God would do something about our situation. We struggle with the situations in our minds and emotions, while we often fail to take advantage of the simplest solution - prayer. We have all been guilty of treating prayer as our last effort to handle our problems. We carry burdens we do not need to bear because we have not REALIZED the power of prayer. We can pray to God and lighten our burdens, but we must pray to God as a first response and not as a last resort. We must earnestly seek Him in our situations, we must have a burning and yearning for our Lord and Savior, a thirst that cannot be quenched with water, but of the Living Water - Jesus. So, before you get all dried out, seek the ultimate thirst quencher, God.

Peace and Blessings

He Lives On The Inside

Ephesians 3:16 (NLT)

Paul's prayer for spiritual growth.

I pray that from His glorious, unlimited resources He will empower you with inner strength through His Spirit.

God lives within us through the power of the Holy Spirit. We must give up things that cause us to forget about His presence or are offensive to Him. We need to make sure our innate lives are engaged in things that please and honor God's presence. We should wake up every day and say in our hearts, "Good morning, God. I want you to feel at home and be comfortable in me." Take care of your temple, inside and out.

Peace and Blessings

Fullness

Ephesians 3:19 (NLT)

May you experience the love of Christ, though it is too great to understand fully. Then you will be made complete with all the fullness of life and power that comes from God.

When we are in the union with Christ and through His empowering Spirit, we are complete. We have all the fullness of God available to us when we have a relationship with Him. Get God and get full!

Peace and Blessings

Praise & Worship

When you need to hear God's voice, praise and worship Him.

Whatever you are praying for, one of the best ways to start is with praise and worship. They will keep your heart right before God and make a way for you to hear His voice and for change to take place. When we enter into respectful, heartfelt praise and worship, God manifests His presence and power to His children; and when His presence and power come, we hear His voice, we see miracles, people are healed, lives are changed, and transformation takes place from the inside out.

Now ask yourself this question:

When you talk to God and listen for His voice, aren't you praying primarily because you want some kind of change or transformation in some area of your life?

Peace and Blessings

Love Covers All

Romans 12:12

Rejoicing in hope; patient in tribulation; continuing instant in prayer.

God has not given us a spirit of fear, but of power, and of love, and a sound mind (II Timothy 1:7).

God has given us the tools to prosper through life. God has given us power, power to pray, power to speak against those things that come against us, and power to REJOICE when we follow His Word and believe. God has given us love, love to cover all things, love to walk upright in His name, love to wash away our doubts, love to conquer what God has set out for us, love to be PATIENT and kind, and love to share among each other. God has given us a direct line to speak and commune with Him. He provides the ear for our voice, He provides the manner in which we can establish a rapport with Him, He is omnipresent that we may go to Him anytime, anywhere.

When we hope for something, rejoice in that it is already done. With God all things are possible. When we are in tribulation, be patient, seek God and let Him move in your situation. Pray, pray unceasingly to our God about everything; not just during our turmoil but through the good times too. God loves us, we must exhibit that we love Him back.

Peace and Blessings

Guidance

Colossians 3:2

Set your affections on things above, not on things on the earth.

When we set our sights on things of Heaven and not of worldly things, we are striving to put God's Word into daily practice. When we get discouraged, flustered, angry, sad, or tempted, remember to look to the hills which cometh our help. This means to rely on God's Word to counteract those negative emotions.

Pray before speaking or taking any action. Learn to commune with God all day as to not get caught up in worldly mess. Ask God to guide you, use your kindred spirit to make decisions, take each day and every situation one step at a time.

Peace and Blessings

Weep Joy

Psalms 30:5b (NLT)

Weeping may last through the night, but joy comes in the morning.

We say we have faith in God, but do we really trust Him? We must fully commit to our faith and commit OURSELVES, families, and all we have to God. When we commit, He permits! Encourage yourself, encourage someone else, and most of all give God the praise He is due.

Peace and Blessings

Resist The Devil

James 4:7 (NLV)

So humble yourselves before God. Resist the devil, and he will flee from you.

As we go through life day in and day out, the devil is hard at work with his conniving and cunning ways with the attempt to kill, hurt, or destroy. When we humble (submit) ourselves to God, there is nothing that can defeat us. We must trust in God's power and guidance to see us through. Tell those temptations, trials, and things that are not of Christ, NO!

Resist or refrain from those very things that may give the devil the upper hand. God loves you. Show Him you love Him too.

Peace and Blessings

Like-Mind

Those around us have a profound influence on us, whether it is how we speak or how we act. We must engage in friendships or relationships with those of like-minds. We must engage with those who build us up and not tear us down. Evaluate your friendships or relationships, are they conducive to your spiritual morals or values? Our concern should be that of continued building of faith and not of those thing that deter us from building our faith. I encourage you to make the necessary changes to grow with Christ.

Peace and Blessings

Thankful

God has done so much and given us many blessings. We must show Him thanksgiving and praise at all times and not just during the holiday season. Giving praise is always an appropriate expression of worship to our awesome God.

Reminisce over all the things God has done for you and blessed you with. Reminisce on the things He has allowed to happen that have built you up. Reminisce on the fact that He gave His only begotten Son. Every day is a day to rejoice.

Peace and Blessings

The "Word"

The "Word" is the agent of creation, the source of God's message, and God's law. Because God is the Word, we are nothing without it. If one tries to live without it, they have abandoned the purpose for which they were created.

Question to ponder: Why were you created?

Peace and Blessings

He Is Able

Thankfulness to God should always be on the lips of those whom He has saved. No matter what happens in life, God is able. He is able to bring us through a storm, able to bless abundantly, able to heal the sick and wounded, able to give new birth, able to redeem the sinner or distressed, and able to bring about any change, HE IS ABLE!

Not only is He able, but He also loves us! He loves us so much that He gave His only begotten Son. He loves us enough to give brand new grace and mercy every day, and He loves us unconditionally!

Peace and Blessings

When Tempted...

James 1:13-14 (NLT)

And remember, when you are being tempted, do not say, "God is tempting me." God is never tempted to do wrong, and He never tempts anyone else.

Temptation comes from our own desires, which entices us and drags us away.

God will never tempt us, but He will allow tests. A test is the procedure intended to establish the quality, performance, or reliability of something, especially before it is taken into widespread use. Tests are lessons to be learned, so when we are tested, we need to take heed to the lesson to be learned and GROW from what we have learned. In addition, we must also LEARN to say NO to temptation, or things that are not of God. Get right people, stop complaining and prepare for tests.

Peace and Blessings

Draw Closer

I Corinthians 16:13 (NLT)

Be on guard. Stand firm in the faith. Be courageous. Be strong.

Draw closer to God and do not let cheap substitutes influence your thoughts, decisions, or actions. Resist those very things that are tempting and that do not align with the Word of God. Be keen on the things you think, say, and do. You must be ready for spiritual battle at all times.

We must know God's Word for ourselves and use what we've learned, know how to resist the devil and speak life into ourselves, our situations, and others.

Peace and Blessings

Eternal Life

John 3:36 (NLT)

And anyone who believes in God's Son has eternal life. Anyone who doesn't OBEY the Son will never experience eternal life but remains under God's angry judgment.

If you choose not to obey God's Word, that could be a detrimental decision. With this being said, I pose a question: Why do we fight harder or make it such a task to read and obey God's Word?

Peace and Blessings

Hope

Hope can be defined as a feeling of expectation and desire for a certain thing to happen. We must learn to put our hope in Christ Jesus and Him only. Apart from Jesus our lives are empty, but when we put our hope in Christ, this appeals to His grace and mercy.

I *HOPE* you are giving God the praise and worship He is due.

Peace and Blessings

How Do You Love?

I Corinthians 16:14

And do everything with love.

Without love we sometimes become prideful. We must not lose the manner in which we love. Love is not only shown through affection, but by being on guard (being watchful or alert for any spiritual enemies), standing firm (sticking with what we believe), being courageous (properly dealing with things that may come against us), and being strong (seeking strength of the Holy Spirit). Collectively, all of these attributes cause us to be loving and to conduct ourselves in a loving manner.

Peace and Blessings

Lead Me, Oh Lord!

We must ask God to lead us in His Will and not that of the flesh. When we have fallen short or lost our way, we must reset and get back on the right path that is led by God.

Pray and ask God for guidance. He will never steer you wrong!

Peace and Blessings

Secure

John 14:1-2 (NLT)

Don't let your hearts be troubled. Trust in God, and trust also in Me. There is more than enough room in My Father's home. If this were not so, would I have told you that I am going to prepare a place for you?

When we pray, seek God, or do works, we must have faith and trust. Without faith and trust we lose our connection with God. We must be SECURE in our faith and trust.

Jesus is telling us and has told us that we have eternal life, but eternal life only comes through our faith and trust in HIM. So if we know the end, we must be WILLING to deal with the now. Read your Word, stay prayed up, give God glory, love thy neighbor, and be SECURE in God!

Peace and Blessings

Are You Wild?

When people do not accept divine guidance, they run wild. When we are outside of God's Will or guidance, things fall apart or become rampant. BUT, when we function in the manner that God has set out for us in His Word, we can maintain peace and joy. Proverbs 29:18 tell us, "But whoever obeys the law is joyful" (NLT).

Having God's Word means little if we are not obeying it.

Peace and Blessings

Done In Love

John 15:9 (NLT)

I have loved you even as the Father has loved me. Remain in my love.

When we are obedient and obey God's commandments, we remain in His love. We are to love each other as well. We may not have to give our life as Jesus did on the cross, but we can show our love in listening, helping, encouraging, giving, and praying. Think of who may need this "love" today and show some love!

Peace and Blessings

Be Joyful...

I Thessalonians 5:16-18 (NLT)

Always be joyful. Never stop praying. Be thankful in all circumstances, for this is God's Will for you who belong to Christ Jesus.

Be joyful, never stop praying, and be thankful. These commands should never be overtaken by our circumstances. When we trust in God and His Word, we are able to pray over our circumstances and overcome with joy and thanksgiving. Our prayer is effective.

Peace and Blessings

Here I stand

Life has been "lifing!" I moved to Georgia and graduated with my PhD - I am a Doctor of Philosophy in Psychology, I finally gained decent employment, I lost a few loved ones, supported my son through his trials, some acquaintances were severed, I have struggled in my faith, but yet, here I stand. I stand to say that God has been good to me. No matter what it looked like, what it felt like, God carried me. When I felt like throwing in the towel, God cared for me.

I stand to say that I can walk with my head held high, I can leave pity parties behind because I truly love and trust God. I can look to the future and know that whatever I put my mind to, I can do it. I have taken the many lessons learned and matured in my faith. I am grateful for all my experiences and lessons - had I not had these experiences and lessons, I would not be who I am today - one of God's chosen vessels. Giving all honor and praise to God!

Peace and Blessings

About the Author

D r. Kristi L. Burk is a previous salon owner of Kristyles & Co., certified hair stylist, hair care instructor, event coordinator, paralegal, and real estate agent. Dr. Burk has over 30 years of servicing the public with styles and hair care. She holds four college degrees including an Associate of Applied Science in Legal Assisting, Bachelor of Criminal Justice, and both a Master of Science and Doctor of Philosophy in Psychology. She is an ordained deacon and a member of several leadership groups. Dr. Burk also is a previous high school cheerleading coach, AAU boys basketball team manager, has been published in BodyBasics and Hair World magazines, inducted in Who's Who Black In Columbus, and Who's Who in Executive & Professionals. Dr. Burk has spent the last several years serving in the mental and behavioral health field.

Dr. Burk has a passion to serve the community and help adolescents and young adults pursue their passions. She has worked with victims of domestic violence, the homeless population, and other disenfranchised populations. Dr. Burk also has a passion for spiritually mentoring and educating women.

Dr. Burk is a native of Columbus, Ohio, and a single mother of one son. Dr. Burk enjoys traveling, reading, writing, and loves THE Ohio State University sports. Dr. Burk invites you to indulge in her devotional writings and hopes that you not only smile, but giggle with God.

GIGGLES…She Laughs is designed as a read along companion as you study the Book of Psalms, the Book of Proverbs, and other various scriptures. The book aims to encourage and enlighten.

A note from Dr. Burk...

In my life's journey, I have experienced domestic violence, rejection, the feeling of worthlessness and failure. My shell may not exhibit this, but I have been wounded and felt I never really healed. Compiling my writings and sharing this book has been a jump start to my road of healing. I share my testimony to encourage both women and men, young and old, that whatever life presents, there is healing in God's Word - there is healing in loving yourself, there is healing in smiling, and there is healing in GIGGLING!

www.ingramcontent.com/pod-product-compliance
Lightning Source LLC
Chambersburg PA
CBHW061650120626
46550CB00003B/893